CW00468492

Tom Cole wore many hats during his working life — crocodile hunter, stockman, drover, miner, horsebreaker, station owner, buffalo hunter and coffee grower, to name but a few.

He was born in England in 1906 but left when he was seventeen, travelling to Australia in search of adventure.

His first job was as a station hand in Queensland and it quickly gave him a taste for more. Before long Tom was an expert stockman working throughout northern Queensland, Western Australia and the Northern Territory. His experiences were many – the Overland Telegraph line, the bush race meetings, horsebreaking, then buffalo shooting and crocodile hunting. Along the way Tom befriended many people, among them tribal Aborigines, buffalo shooters and drovers. In his thirties he bought and sold a number of large stations in the Northern Territory – Goodparla, Esmerelda, Ingarrabba and Tandidgee.

Tom's autobiography, *Hell West and Crooked*, was published in 1988 and has since become a bestseller.

Tom Cole died in 1995.

Also by Tom Cole in Sun
Crocodiles and Other Characters

RIDING THE WILDMAN PLAINS

The Letters and Diaries of TOM COLE 1923-1943

SUN
AUSTRALIA

First published 1992 in Macmillan by Pan Macmillan Publishers Australia
First published 1993 in Sun by Pan Macmillan Publishers Australia
This Sun edition published 1994 by Pan Macmillan Australia Pty Limited
St Martins Tower, 31 Market Street, Sydney

Reprinted 1994, 1996, 1997

National Library of Australia
cataloguing-in-publication data:

Cole, Tom 1906-1995
Riding the wildman plains: the diaries and letters of Tom Cole 1923-1943.

ISBN 0 7251 0740 5

1. Cole, Tom, 1906-1995. 2. Cole, Tom, 1906-1995 - Correspondence
3. Cole, Tom, 1906-1995 - Diaries. 4. Stockmen - Northern Territory -
Correspondence. 5. Stockmen - Northern Territory - Diaries. 6. Stockmen -
Northern Territory - Biography. 7. Frontier and pioneer life - Northern Territory.
I. Title.

994.29042092

Printed in Australia by McPherson's Printing Group

FOREWORD

In his best-selling autobiography *Hell West and Crooked* Tom Cole has given us a splendid account of raw pioneering life in Australia's far north in the 1920s and 30s, when he was a stockman and horsebreaker. His ability to recall accurately the events of those days was aided by his own diaries and the letters he wrote to his mother in England after he arrived in Australia in 1923, all of seventeen years of age.

Now we are fortunate enough to have *Riding the Wildman Plains*, a collection of those letters and personal diary entries. This is a window into twenty years of Australian northern outback life from 1923–43. Tom Cole was never interested in self aggrandisement. The teenage adventurer began as, and continued to be, a thoughtful, honest and colourful diarist. He was a keen observer of his time. The realities of the day are reflected in his references to Aborigines as blacks, natives, boys and lubras. Yet those who read his diaries and letters will be aware Tom Cole was no racist. He took people as he found them.

The descriptions of everyday life in the stock camps — the humour, danger, boredom and bizarre — are featured in these contemporary accounts. The day-to-day diaries are often laconic, with entries like 18 August, 1934:

Went foot shooting today and was jammed up between a couple of bulls — things were very touchy for a few seconds.

But because he was writing of a life unimaginable to his mother in England, his careful scene-setting and vivid descriptions to her augment the sparse prose of his personal diaries. Knowing the pathological English fear of snakes and spiders imagined to inhabit every crevice of the Antipodes, it is difficult to imagine Mrs Cole being reassured by part of her son's letter of 12 December, 1935, describing a moonlight camp near Pine Creek in the Northern Territory:

About half past nine or ten, Fred gave a blood-curdling yell and broke all existing records for the high jump, long jump and then 100 yards dash. I didn't know whether it was a ghost or hostile blacks. Looking over to his swag I could see coiled up and gleaming in the bright moonlight a snake fully seven feet long. Fred's yell soon brought the boys down from the camp and with a stick they quickly killed it. We found it to be a Darwin Brown, one of the deadliest snakes in the world.

Tom Cole's diaries and letters are published as they were originally written, with an occasional brief explanation comment from the author. They stand alone as a fascinating contemporary narrative.

TIM BOWDEN
SYDNEY, 1992

PREFACE

These diaries and letters will appear to many readers disjointed, lacking in detail and continuity. There are very good reasons for this. In the first place I never imagined that I would be writing books or that my diaries would ever appear in print. Had I thought so, I would have recorded more detail! As it is, the diaries are confined to bare essentials and I can only hope that the reader finds them interesting.

Keeping diaries was a vital part of an outback cattleman's job, whether he was a headstockman, an overseer or a manager, and if and when he left, the diary would be handed over to whoever took over. The diaries were a means of keeping a check on the date, branding figures, the state of waterholes, what horses were being worked, and a hundred and one other details of stock camp life. But at the same time, because of the pressures of working stock camp, the entries were kept to a minimum.

Looking back over the long span of years from the comfort of a Sydney flat, the way of life on that land at the back of beyond seems quite remarkable and not without a touch of insanity. At the time, of course, it seemed perfectly normal to me because, I suppose, everybody was living that kind of life. The men I rode with were all, without exception, great men, straight as a gun barrel. The Aborigines, too, were great horsemen and flawless trackers, and without them we would never have managed. Without these unsung heroes of the outback this book would not have been possible.

TOM COLE
SYDNEY, 1992

ACKNOWLEDGEMENTS

I wish to record my very sincere thanks to Tim Bowden for his very generous foreword and to the Australian Institute of Aboriginal and Torres Strait Islander Studies Pictorial Collection for their help in providing copies of many of my photographs.

1923–1931

At seventeen I decided to take up the offers of the posters that beckoned young empire builders to the colonies. It was not a difficult decision. As the eldest son in a family of eight I was not particularly endeared to my father. With the help of my Uncle George and my mother it was all arranged.

S.S. ORMUZ,
ENGLISH CHANNEL

1923

Dear Mum and everybody

I expect you will be surprised to hear from me so soon. I had no idea I could post a letter so quickly, but it appears that we drop the Pilot off at 10 o'clock and he will take letters and mail from the passengers.

I arrived on the boat by tug, as she was lying off, about 10.30. It is 8.15 now and we passed Dover about an hour ago, so we are well into the channel. There is a tidy swell but I don't feel a bit seasick.

Dinner was served at 12.30 and the food was very good — we had soup, fried potatoes, gravy, meat and rice pudding. For tea we had gravy, meat, bread and butter, jam-cake and cocoa.

Thankyou for the £1 note, which was very welcome. I can't write a letter to anybody else because of the shortage of stamps. I am one of the fortunate few who has had a stamp promised them (I hope I get it).

My address: T. Cole, c/– Immigration Officer, Brisbane, Queensland.

Tell Peg to tell Arthur, Tom, Ken and co. why I couldn't write for a while.

Love to Peg, Hilda, Norman, John, Phil, Len and not forgetting you, also Auntie Emmie and Grandma.

Your loving Tom

S.S. ORMUZ,
INDIAN OCEAN

15 SEPTEMBER 1923

Dear Peg

By the time you receive this I shall have settled down more or less in Queensland and hope to have received a letter from you. At the present time of writing, I have three weeks voyage before me as we are still in the Indian Ocean. Today is Tuesday and we get into Fremantle on Thurs. Sept. 20.

I went ashore at Colombo and enjoyed myself more than at any other port. I went with Mr Richardson, the immigration officer whom we met at Australia House. Colombo is a ripping place full of tropical plants. The birds in this country are magnificent and the butterflies gorgeously coloured and as big as my two hands.

Our coolie said he would take us to see a Buddhist temple. On the way we saw an Indian snake charmer and we stopped. He had a rush-basket with about four cobras in it and with a funny looking affair he played weird music, not unlike bag-pipes. The largest snake (about 8 feet) he called Charley. He made them dance and fight and when he stopped playing they all went back into their baskets. Sometimes he let all of 'em crawl around his neck.

We had the whole day in Colombo, but I went back about four to have a swim as we were allowed to bathe off the ship. It gets dark very quickly about 6.30. We sailed about 9 p.m.

Your loving brother

THORNLANDS
WEST CLEVELAND
QUEENSLAND

OCTOBER 1923

Dear Mum

Received your letter with two of Peg's. All three of them were waiting for me when I arrived because we were three days late — just as we got to the Brisbane River we had to anchor owing to the denseness of smoke from bush fires.

The officer I was friendly with on board recommended me to the immigration officer at Brisbane and I had the first choice of jobs. I have chosen one at Cleveland, as you can see by my address, and I have a splendid job.

My boss's name is Major Campbell and he is a jolly fine fellow. I have got a room to myself in a house where a married couple live, who are employed on the farm, which by the way is a fruit farm. I have my meals in the same house as the Campbells. The food is splendid and I am extremely comfortable and wouldn't change my job with anybody. The Major by the way is married and has a charming wife and four children, whose ages range from one baby in arms to a boy of five years.

I was very fortunate indeed in getting such a job. I am only 23 miles from the town and the Major brought me from Brisbane in his car. Although it is quite near to the town, it is quite wild here. We have the bush at the back and our nearest neighbour is about a quarter of a mile away, which is quite civilised for Australia.

On the farm they grow some very strange fruits, papaws, custard apples and a funny fruit with a Latin name, which in English is mysterious delicious.

Papaws are a very strange fruit, they look like marrows growing on trees. Custard apples are equally strange, the skin is like the skin of a cucumber, it is round and grows as large as a small football and tastes like custard.

Everything is very strange here. It gets dark at 6.30 at present, but will be an hour later in the summer. I usually go to

ORIENT   LINE.

BETWEEN ENGLAND AND AUSTRALIA.

Managers—ANDERSON, GREEN & CO., LTD., FENCHURCH AVENUE, LONDON, E.C. 3.

PASSENGERS BOOKED FOR
Gibraltar, Toulon, Naples, Port
Said, Suez, Colombo, Fremantle,
Adelaide, Melbourne, Sydney,
Brisbane and all Chief Ports in
Australia, Tasmania, and New
Zealand.

On board the S.S.

Hornlands   192

West Cleveland

Queensland

Dear Mum

Ever so pleased to
hear you got a holiday, received your
letter with two of Pegs all three
of them were waiting for me when
I arrived as we were three days
late also just as we got to the
the river Brisbane we had to anchor
owing to the denseness of smoke from
bush fires.

The officer I was
friendly with on board reccommended
me to the Immigration officer at
Brisbane + I had the first choice
of jobs + I have chosen one at
Cleveland as you see by my address

bed at 8 o'clock. Nobody wants to stay up later as the heat of the day combined with the day's work makes one very tired. Of course retiring early I don't feel like staying in bed after 6.30, even on Sunday, when I have nothing to do before breakfast, which is at 7.30, except feed two cows and sometimes catch a horse and harness it for the day's work. The horses are turned loose into the paddock, which is half bush.

My wages are 15 shillings a week and I get 5 shillings for myself. But there is nothing I want money for as shops are unknown, so I told the Major that I am not going to the trouble to draw it. I think I shall be able to clothe myself without drawing on the immigration people and then my passage money will be paid off in less than a year. After four months I get a half crown rise, the Major said.

I get a day and a half off a week. Sat. and Sun. I have free to do my own washing, so I make Sunday morning my washing day and the foreman's wife, who is ever so good to me, does my ironing and keeps my room tidy. The foreman is a jolly good fellow.

Everything in the garden is lovely. I have plenty to do in my spare time without spending money. We are about a quarter of a mile from the sea and I can go swimming and the Major gave me a fishing rod so I can fish. Also, I have a horse to catch on Sunday, which is running about in the bush somewhere, and I shall be able to ride it as much as I like. The boss also has a rifle that he has given me the use of and on Saturday we are going on a kangaroo hunt.

So you see I have a good job, have got with a good family, like the country and am very comfortable. So I will close, love to all and remember me to uncles.

Your loving son

Thornlands
West Cleveland

November 1923

Dear Peg

A Merry Xmas and all that and I hope you'll like the enclosed, although it isn't a very useful affair. You see — Mrs Campbell got it for me in Brisbane and, as we are more or less 'Out Back', I haven't got a chance to buy anything, although I think you can buy hair oil and shaving brushes at the butcher in Cleveland. The bird on the calendar, which is for Grandma and Auntie with my best wishes, is a Laughing Jackass or Kookaburra; at sunset and sunrise they laugh, heaven knows what at, and the row is enough to make you cry.

I don't know whether I've written to you before, anyhow if I have I've forgotten. I received two of your letters at the immigration depot, both were waiting for me. Got my job coming from the boat to Brisbane in the tram. I was the first chap to get a job. I had a jolly good choice, so I chose a fruit-farming job at Cleveland and live in a house or rather a bungalow with another fellow.

The Campbells are a topping crowd and I am very comfortable and have everything I wish for. The house is on a ridge and overlooks the sea, which is about half a mile away, so I have the sea for swimming and fishing, the bush at the back for shooting wallabies and kangaroos and the farm for working. So you see I have everything I wish for except girls and if they were here I don't think I could spare much time for them. 'Seven days shalt thou labour and do all thy work and the eighth day thou shalt start all over again'.

On the farm we grow custard apples, papaws, lemons, oranges, pineapples, a few tomatoes and cucumbers. We've a large paddock, which is a portion of bush fenced off, where you can easily get lost. The horses are kept in this paddock and it is quite an afternoon's or morning's enjoyment catching 'em.

This is a very bad time just now as there is a serious drought on. The tropical rains are over three months overdue and everybody, including ourselves, is hard at work on irrigation.

I don't think there is much more news at present. I can't write very long letters as I have about two dozen to write, about a week to do it in and very little time to myself. We start at dawn and finish at dark and feel pretty tired. It is hard work compared with home but I like it very much out here. I've signed on this farm for a year, so I'm here for that long anyhow. I may go up north later as I don't think I shall go in for fruit seriously — you want such a terrible lot of capital and a dry season can easily ruin a farmer.

Goodbye and love to all, a Merry Xmas and a Happy New Year.

Yours ever

MALENY
QUEENSLAND
1924

... there is only two of us running a 150 acre farm, milking between 50 to 60 cows twice a day, with three cultivation paddocks, one of which is easily six times bigger than his (Major Campbell's) bit of garden.

A week or so ago we dipped a mob of about 60 cattle; this is for the purpose of keeping down the ticks that live on the beasts. The place where we dip is about a mile away on a neighbouring farm. We had to go through a boundary fence, the opening was rather on the small side, and a crowd broke away and rushed down the fence towards a creek. I put my horse to a gallop in an attempt to head them off. Just as I got within about ten yards of the fence, my bridal rein broke. It rather put the wind up me as I had no control whatever over the animal and there wasn't much time to think. I did what I considered to be the best thing. I chucked myself off and landed quite safely, but rather forcibly, in a patch of ferns. Coming back, I was shutting a fence and carelessly didn't tie the horse up — he cleared off for his life home, so I had to walk the rest of the way.

There was a bit of excitement the other day: we were killing and had a rather wild beast. He was lassoed by the horn and then broke away down the paddock. Two or three rounded him up again, near the place where we kill. One fellow on foot grabbed the rope and attempted to hold him, evidently twisting the rope round his hand trying to get a better hold, but pretty quickly dropped it with a couple of broken fingers. In the meantime, the beast had broken back and got underneath a horse, which was snorting and kicking like blazes until somebody sorted them out with the aid of a stock whip.

My duties are something like this: rise 4.30; get engine and milking machines ready; by this time the cows are up, get cows into the top yard, bring cows in and get them ready for the machines; start engine and start milking; milking finishes about 8.30; feed pigs and calves; breakfast; after breakfast, it is usually getting horses ready for anything that is going; at present I'm ploughing.

Have just received your letter enclosing 10 shilling note, thanks very much, it's the wisest thing you could possibly have thought of. I want to save as much money as possible, so I have cut out smoking and am trying to keep myself in clothes on my 5 shillings per week and have so far succeeded, although I have been here nearly four months. I have only been out two evenings. Christmas Eve I went into Maleny and spent 5 shillings in riotous living and I spent an evening at Mr Gibson's brother's place, so you see I don't spend much money.

It is early autumn here and everybody is rushing around getting their cattle ready for the show, which is in April. We are putting a lot of cattle in it, so one way or another we have plenty to do.

Unfortunately, I lost a few things on the boat as somebody burst open one of the hinges of my tin trunk. They tried the lock but couldn't manage it. Anyhow, the ship's plumber soon fixed it up for me.

ENROUTE TO RUTHERGLEN STATION

APRIL 1925

Dear Peggy

I forget how long ago it is since I last wrote to you but things
have been happening since then. I left Warner's as I had a job
offered to me at Mitchell on a station. Mitchell, I might tell
you, is 875 miles from Brisbane. I am on my way there now, so
this letter is being written in the train — still, I'd better start at
the beginning.

I got down to Brisbane on Easter Monday at about 6 o'clock
after a delightful ride (about 12 miles) down the Blackall Range
on the bonnet of a Hudson car. I also stood all the way to
Brisbane (about sixty miles) in the train. Anyhow, I managed
to find some decent digs. I made arrangements to leave Brisbane for Mitchell for the following Friday. I had about 15 quid
clear, so I made a very successful attempt to dispose of some of
it.

Of course after 12 months in the bush I hadn't a rag
practically, so quite a lot of my money went that way. I went to
five or six shows and also managed to fill in odd time by going
for a spin up the river and doing a bit of surfing. It was one of
the most pleasant holidays that I can remember — there's
nothing like the bush to make one appreciate civilisation.

My next job is a cowboy's and I think the station is sheep
and cattle . . . (Couldn't continue this owing to the speed of the
train; the Western Mail does a modest seventy.)

I arrived in Mitchell at 8.30 on Saturday morning and from
there I went about 120 miles south by car to a place called
Homeboin Station, where I am at present, but this is not my
destination. I have to go another 30 miles west to Rutherglen
Station, where I shall work, and I am waiting for someone to
come for me and take me from here to there.

I have been here since Saturday and today is Wednesday. I
have been helping the chaps here muster and draft cattle, as
well as mustering, drafting, branding and breaking-in horses.
I've been helping a chap named Brown to break-in five. We

put the ropes on them Monday; the mouthing tackle, or 'jewellery' as we call it, on Tuesday; on Wednesday all five had the saddle on and were ridden. Three of them just rooted and reefed around a bit and then quietened down, but the other two, gee! I rode one of them — a black filly with two white hind socks. The first time I got on her — I had my foot in the stirrup and was just cocking my leg over when something happened! It was quite all right till I hit the ground, then I saw planets.

RUTHERGLEN
VIA ST GEORGE
QUEENSLAND

21 JUNE 1925

Dear Mum

I received your letter last mail and was very glad to get one from you after such a long time.

So you really and truly want me to come home, well if that's the case I'll come, but not straight away. I don't think you need send me any money as I should soon have my passage money. By the time this letter reaches you I should have somewhere between 30 and 40 pounds. I am getting £10 a month and keep (I got £2 a month rise after I had been here a fortnight). Up to the present I have been more than keeping myself in clothes by trapping rabbits and shooting kangaroos for their pelts (they are worth a fair bit now) — so you see that is a tenner a month clear.

I would like to come home with about £100 apart from my passage.

I wouldn't work my passage under any circumstances whatever, I have seen the conditions under which sailors live. Don't you think it would be rather a good idea to come home with some money?

I don't want you to be worried over the way I am wandering about, everybody does it out here. Furthermore, I am in a new country and I want to see it.

I have got a splendid job here with a fine family and I am at present very comfortable. The hours are shorter and I have Saturday afternoon and Sunday off. Just lately I have been spending the weekends with a couple of friends, whose father has just started them on a sheep station, and coming on back to Rutherglen on Monday. We practically live in the saddle at Rutherglen and it is a great life. When we are not using the horses, we are running about the station in an old Ford — a most decrepit affair, stayed and strutted up with fencing wire.

Next week or the week after, I have five young horses to break in. They are in the smallest paddock on the place (7000 acres), they are fearfully wild and we are anticipating some fun in yarding them alone. I think that it will be easier than riding 'em, though. I have picked out the best of the bunch, a black filly, and have bought her for £2. I don't think I will have any difficulty in getting £6 for her when she is broken.

We are now in the middle of winter here and I sleep under a single blanket and wear a pair of light trousers and just a shirt, boots (riding) and socks of course. In the summer the temperature goes up to 120°F, it is 51° now.

I am glad I left Maleny as they used to get such a lot of rain there. It was raining when I left — I had a letter from Bodley two mails (weeks) ago and a letter from Warner's last mail — it is still raining.

Before I leave Australia, if I do, I want to see the Barron Falls in North Queensland. Most probably, I will come home via the Panama and the South Sea Islands, Honolulu, etc. So if you really need me I'll come; after a winter averaging 50°F the English winter will take some sticking.

Please write as often as you can. You can have no idea how much I welcome a letter.

Don't worry over me any more as I can see you are doing.

Love to everybody, your loving son

% Taylor & Reid
Rutherglen
St George
Qld
Australia

Sat   25 Aug

Dear Mum
      I received another
terrible letter from you last mail. I
do wish you wouldnt worry about
me so. I always get my mail safley
as I notify the postal authoritys, in
spite of the fact that the Daily Mail
is addressed
      % R J Bodley
        Via Queensboro
         Qld
          Australia
There isnt such a place as Queensboro
in australia so the P.O. only had
my name & Bodleys to go by &
Queensland to search for me in. No, I
dont think you need worry about my
mail anyway, & as for my
addresses, well you'll have a lot
of grey hairs if you let a detail like

RUTHERGLEN

SATURDAY, 25 AUGUST 1925

Dear Mum

I received another terrible letter from you last mail. I do wish you wouldn't worry about me so. I always get my mail safely as I notify the postal authorities, in spite of the fact that you have addressed the Daily Mail newspapers: C/- R J Bodley Via Queensboro Qld Australia. There isn't such a place as Queensboro in Australia, so the PO only had my name and Bodley's to go by and Queensland to search for me in. No, I don't think you need worry about my mail anyway — as for my addresses, well, you'll have a lot of grey hairs if you let a detail like that worry you.

There's a mob of 2000 fat bullocks going to Ningin from Homeboin, one of our neighbours, which is about 700 miles and it's possible that I'm going with them. A drover gets £4 10s and keep per week and it is a seven week trip in a good season. Then there's a possibility of me going up to the Northern Territory later.

We've been pretty busy here this last week. About a year ago the fence was broken down and a lot of Homeboin cattle got in — we've been mustering for them. They are a particularly wild lot of cattle and it isn't without its thrills; needless to say, they get very flighty when they see a stockyard. Another fellow and I were bringing up a mob and spent a lot of time trying to coax them through the gate — whips were cracking but it only seemed to make them worse — then a big bullock broke. I galloped out to wheel him and was just coming round on his shoulder, when my horse went in between two trees and my leg got one of 'em. Well, for the next two hours it was completely numb and after that it was pretty sore — take it from me.

The next day, Friday, we finished the mustering and in the afternoon we started to draft them off, the Homeboin's from the Rutherglen's, when a storm broke. The ground got greasy and the horses didn't like it, at all. I was riding Danger, a smart sort of a colt, round the outside of the yards in case anything jumped out as the yards were in a bad condition, and the improbable happened. A bullock smashed a rail round the opposite side to where I was — didn't I whip those spurs into Danger and didn't he travel. I got round him (the bullock) three times and turned him, and three times he beat me. I was just turning him for the fourth time when I felt the horse slip under me. I tried to pull him round, but too late — we both hit the ground a terrific crack — fortunately, neither of us were hurt. It eventually took three men to yard that bullock.

I've been doing a bit of shooting lately, with no little degree of success. Last Sunday I shot seven emus, three kangaroos, a rabbit and an eagle. The eagle had a wing spread of 7 feet 6 inches — there is half a crown on its head as they do a great deal of damage to the lambs.

If I do not go droving, I shall be very busy here for the next few weeks mustering sheep.

I hope you will write a bit more often, you've no idea how a letter is appreciated out here. I have even written to firms for catalogues and quotations that I don't want just to get a letter. We only get mail once a week.

Love to everybody, your loving son

RUTHERGLEN

15 OCTOBER 1925

Dear Mum

I received your letter last mail and was pleased to get such an informative letter, but there's still a dickens of a lot I would like to know.

Doubtless you remember me telling you in a previous letter that I anticipated either going droving or going to the Northern Territory. Well, I had the offer of a good job on one of the biggest cattle stations in Australia. It is in the Northern Territory. I am leaving for Lake Nash (the name of the station) in about a fortnight.

This should prove a pretty big thing for me as the name Northern Territory is a qualification in itself. I am looking forward with great expectations to my next change and hope to settle for some time. In any event, I shall for a certainty be there for a year as the Queensland National Pastoral Company (the owners) pay my fare out there only if I stay in their employ for 12 months. As the fare is £20, I think I can safely say that I shall be there 12 months. So here's luck to the Northern Territory.

I will try to get somebody to take my photo and send you one. I am a bit taller and a bit broader but for all that pretty lean and very sunburnt and fairly wiry. Nobody seems to put on any fat in the terrific heat that we get in the summer. Although this is spring, the shade reading was well over 100°F three weeks ago.

When I leave here I am sending away a pile of kangaroo skins to Brisbane, which I hope will net a tenner, although I expect the bottom will drop out of the market when I send my parcel down. Anyhow, I've picked a few skins out and hope to have them tanned and will send them to you as soon as this operation is completed. I think there will be a fox skin, an emu skin and a kangaroo skin; all the proceeds of my rifle except the fox, which I trapped.

By the way would anybody like to make me a present of a pair of rubber tennis shoes, the white crepe rubber variety. These cannot be procured under about 3 shillings out here. I haven't bought much in the way of clothes since I've been out here and consequently I want a completely new outfit — I was totting up a list the other day and it clean put the wind up me. Looks as though all my hard-earned savings are going up in lovely blue smoke. In fact, if I manage to keep twenty quid, I'll be lucky.

Well cheerio, write you some more from NT.

Love to everybody, your affectionate son

ST GEORGE

1 NOVEMBER 1925

Dear Peg

I have now left Rutherglen for good as I prophesied earlier and I am now on my way to Brisbane, prior to leaving for the Northern Territory where I have an excellent job awaiting me.

I left Rutherglen yesterday. Deshons, who are Rutherglen neighbours and friends of mine, were going to Dirrinbandi but offered to run me in to go to St George (about 30 miles out of their way).

I shall leave here for Thallon by the coach on Monday, from where I will catch the train to Brisbane. I'll get in to Brisbane on Tuesday and leave on the following Friday for Lake Nash Station, Northern Territory — nearly 1000 miles from Brisbane.

Will write again and let you know how I am getting on.

Love to everybody, your affec. brother

LAKE NASH STATION,
NORTHERN TERRITORY
VIA URANDANGIE
QUEENSLAND

DECEMBER 1925

Dear Len

As you see by the above address, I am now enjoying(?) life in the Northern Territory. This is one of the most uninhabited places in the world and the most uninhabited of Australia. I don't know how much bigger than Europe it is, but it's a goodish bit.

There are 29 police up here (mounted) and I think according to the last census there are less than 1000 whites. White women are as rare as celluloid cats in June.

I have been here a month now and when I left Rutherglen to come here, it took me a week and altogether I travelled 2100 miles, which includes breaking my journey with a day here and there.

Lake Nash is a fair lump of a station, all open plain country, and if you get a modern map of Queensland you can see it marked on the small bit of the Northern Territory, which is usually enclosed on the aforesaid map. It's on the Georgina River, which at present, like all the other rivers and creeks, is completely dry. The size of the station is 5000 square miles, and it has about 40 000 head of cattle and 700 horses. It is worked by two stock-camps. I was until yesterday in number one camp, where they are living out on the run all through the year, mustering for bullocks, cows and calves, and branding horses, etc. There are no fences except for a couple of horse paddocks which are each about 5 miles square.

There is a bit of a drought on at present — the wet season, for some reason or other, is behind schedule. All creeks, rivers, waterholes, etc. are dry, consequently the stock are dependent on artificial water supplies, to wit sub-artesian bores. There are 20 bores here, the majority are driven by steam-engines, one by oil and odd ones by windmills.

I have just been taken out of the stock-camp to pump at No. 17 bore Arga-darga-da (all the bores have blackfellow names) until the drought breaks, when I shall go back into the stock-camp.

Arga-darga-da is at the back of the run, which is 92 miles from the head station. The head station is a couple of hundred miles from a town and about 300 from a railway; Brisbane the nearest city is nearly 2000 miles away. We are scheduled to get a mail once a week — we're lucky to get it once a fortnight, but usually it comes once in three weeks and in the wet season it comes once in three months. Read Mrs Gunn's book *We of the Never-Never*, it deals with the NT. The character, 'The Sanguine Scot', now has a pub in Darwin. A barman he had working for him was kicking around St George where I struck him, so I have, you might say, a passing interest in the book.

If it doesn't rain before Xmas I shall be pumping for water on the 25th. I shall have a couple of blackfellows out there (a bit of company). I shall probably shoot a turkey (the plain turkeys are much better eating than the domestic ones). I shot three yesterday, one of which I cooked today so you see the prospect of spending a Merry Xmas is a very remote contingency.

There's only the horses left to talk and write about now — they are a pretty bad lot. About once a month the camps go in to the station for fresh horses and that's the time to see bucking exhibitions. Each man takes three or four horses into the stock-camp from the fresh horse paddock, and for a week the horses buck all day. At the end of the day a lot of 'em are spitting blood — I've had my share of it all. I got thrown five times in one day, a week ago.

I suppose you will be reading this letter in a shade lower temperature than the one I am writing it in. The shade reading about ten minutes ago was 118°F.

With regard to you leaving the army, think carefully before you act. The work out here is very hard. It sounds all right riding horses all day, but I can assure you it is hard work, especially with the temperature like it is just now. Branding is terribly hard, and I have never in my life done anything more gruelling than riding a rough-horse (we call it a buckjumper) as you can well imagine when the rider spits blood. There is a certain element of danger with it. A week ago one of the men went away with a broken knee, the result of a bullock charge in the branding yard; a fellow in the other stock-camp went away with a broken collarbone and two ribs. He was thrown over a horse's head and the horse galloped over him. A friend of mine, who is driving the steam engine at the next bore, is forbidden to ride for a year because he was thrown from his horse onto a stump and tore the muscle of his right leg. He's got a scar about 10 inches long and walks with a limp. The living is rough, although healthy. There is plenty of food, although plain. When the stockmen have finished a day's work they roll themselves up in a blanket or mosquito net in the hot weather. I have not seen a white woman for a month and don't expect to see one for another three or four.

I don't want to put you off coming, but the above are the

plain unvarnished facts as I have found them. As you know I have tried other branches of life on the land, but don't recommend them; the present one suits me. Another branch that I hope to try is droving or overlanding cattle. Mobs of anything from 700 to 2000 go down to Aardoch Station (a station belonging to the same firm that I now work for, The Queensland National Pastoral Company) and fat cattle are droved down there once a year and from there they are trucked to the markets.

Droving pay is £5 a week and keep and as it is a 13 week trip, there would be a nice little cheque at the end of it — then a cove can always go back to his station until next season.

In the country people never pay their men by the week or month. Now take my case: if I want anything from Brisbane. I send down for it and get the boss to put in a cheque for the amount, then when I leave I draw a lump sum.

Out here the men booze fearfully, the usual procedure being for a fellow to go into the bush until he has a cheque for about £200, then go to a pub, put the cheque in and tell them to chuck him out when it's gone.

Lake Nash

January 1926

Dear Mum

Have just received two letters dated November 1st and 11th. By the seem of it, I must have missed some of yours as this was the first time I had heard of Donald being ill. You don't seem to think it's very serious — in the latter of the two letters you say that you hope to have him home for Xmas — so I am not worrying. Regarding my letters not reaching you inside two months, I can quite understand it. Rutherglen is about 500 miles from Brisbane, with the mail service being weekly and mail boats departing fortnightly for England. From Rutherglen the mail goes 5 miles by packhorse and then 200 miles by car across the plains, so they could easily, and often did, get stuck in rainy weather. Therefore, it could easily be a month before the letter left Brisbane for England.

Lake Nash where I am at present, although it is in the Territory, the mail comes via Urandangie (soft 'g') and from there to the 'Lake'. There is no regular mail service and we depend upon lorries and teams (bullocks, horses, camels) for our mail. I have had two mail deliveries in two and a half months; the second one arrived yesterday and I am not expecting another for a month or so. The teams aren't absolutely busting to come out this way — water's too scarce. One bloke started out on a motorbike. He went wrong and they found him two days later with his tongue the size of a melon, drinking lubricating oil. I didn't hear whether he recovered.

I haven't received the parcel yet but am hoping to next mail and thanks very much for it. I spent my Xmas at the bore watering thirsty cattle. For dinner I had salt beef, bread and tinned pineapple, which a thoughtful station supplied for the occasion. The temperature was 115°F in the shade and,

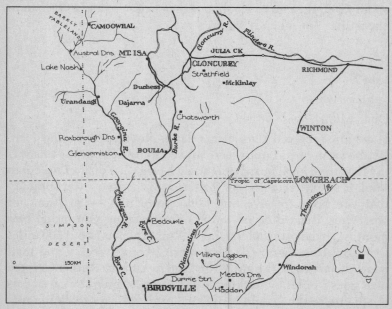

although it might sound strange, we (my mate and I) didn't know it was Xmas day — as a matter of fact we had been arguing about it. I reckoned it was Boxing Day and my mate reckoned Xmas was a couple of days ago. However, someone arrived with a couple of tins of fruit, a few rations and also some books from the station circulating library, and announced that it was Xmas day.

It's been very difficult to get a photo of myself up to the present. Tons of chaps have taken it but I have never received one. However, I was in Townsville recently and went for a trip to Magnetic Island on the Great Barrier Reef where a fellow took my photo with a postcard size camera. I bought the film off him and if it turns out all right I'll send it to you. The results should be here in the next mail. Magnetic Island is a very pretty place, complete with coconut palms, coral beach, surf, and hundreds of pomegranates growing wild.

It's been very disappointing trying to save money. When I left Rutherglen I had nearly £50, which I had been pinching and scraping to save. Consequently, I was very short of clothes, in fact, I had practically none. They are terribly dear out here, and by the time I had finished buying the clothes I had made a very substantial hole in my savings. However I hope to recover my financial equilibrium very shortly. You don't want to worry about my change of address. It's rather a good idea this travelling business as all my expenses are paid and very liberally, too. I travelled first class and stayed at the Queens Hotel, Townsville, while waiting for the North Western connection, and that is one of the best hotels in Australia. They charged 30 shillings a day and I had £2 left over, which went into my personal exchequer.

I have not definitely decided to stay in this country permanently — I cannot say either way yet. If I do come home it won't be for a year or so and I will have a bit of money.

When I leave pumping and go back into the stock-camp I shan't have much time to write. The bullock muster begins shortly and that means a lot of night work, for which of course we get paid extra. This is a huge run and the cattle have to be watched at night because yards are few and far between and sometimes the mob is too big to go into a yard, anyway. Four thousand is not an unusual number of cattle.

Well, cheerio — got to do some cooking — am quite a culinary artist and can cook anything from wind pie to charcoal on toast.

Love to Donald — tell him to hurry up and get better.

Your loving son

LAKE NASH

FEBRUARY 1926

Dear Mum

Just received your Xmas box in excellent condition and it couldn't have come at a better time. Many thanks for it. Some obliging customs Johnny cleaned up all the chocs.

A lot of things have happened since I last wrote. At present, another fellow and I have a contract to supply a bore with wood to use in a steam-engine. The contract is for £250. We hope to make about £5 a week clear.

We are working terribly hard, harder than I've ever worked before. Consequently, I haven't much time to write.

Many happy returns to Peg on her 21st birthday. I haven't seen the boss for three weeks, otherwise I would have got a cheque from him to send her (we are 65 miles from the head station). My 20th birthday came and went without fuss.

As soon as work eases off, I'm going to put the hard word on the boss for a week's spell and then I'll have a big write up, so look out in about six weeks time.

The weather is terribly hot. Swinging a 4 pound axe with a 110°F shade temperature is a guaranteed weight reducer.

We are living like fighting cocks. The only disadvantage is the absence of milk, eggs and vegetables. Everything is tinned. If we only had fresh vegetables 'I wouldn't call the king my uncle'. However, it can't do me much harm as I'm over 6 feet and still growing both ways (up and out).

I haven't slept in a bed or under a roof (except the stars) or seen a white woman for four months. It's a healthy life and I'm pretty hard.

I find that I can't save ten pounds a month in the first place. Some bright 'erb, who calls himself a member of parliament, decided that compared with the standard of living stockman's wages were too high so he reduced them. Also, I had been pinching and scraping for so long that I had hardly a rag to stand up in and, clothes being so darned dear, a new rig-out cost me a goodish bit. However, I'm doing all right now. One advantage of living in the bush is that one doesn't need any glad rags. On the other hand, when there are those rare occasions that call for such glad rags I find I have grown out of most things. Last time I was in Brisbane I took a 15½ inch collar and when I left England I took a fourteen, so I s'pose next time it will be a 16½ inch. Anyhow, after wearing an open shirt for so long, it's a fair cow having to wear a collar and tie. Just at present, I've got a three months growth, in fact, a real live beard, with a splash of bright red in it. It reminds one of a red sea sunset and as it puts about ten years on me, I'm quite proud of it.

Well so long — keep everybody up to scratch with letters — don't forget those tennis shoes, size 8.

Those skins I was going to send you went bush completely. Some railway Johnny wrote me a letter and said that the whole railway system of Queensland was dislocated in an ineffectual attempt to find 'em, so that's that I s'pose. Anyhow, I'll shoot some more for you. Well cheers.

Your affectionate son

LAKE NASH STATION

9 MARCH 1926

Dear Mum

I received your letter of the 11th January yesterday. The Station mail has been held up at Urandangie, hence the delay.

I think it is doubtful whether you could get anything for me at home as you see, starting with boots —

The boots that are worn are elastic-sided riding boots with 2½ inch heels. They are necessary because if you wear ordinary boots it is possible that the low heel will slip through the stirrup iron — if thrown from the horse (one is absolutely certain to be thrown several times a month). The low heel can be caught in the stirrup iron — if the rider is then dragged about, anything might happen. A blackfellow got caught like this and while being dragged along the ground the horse was kicking out at him — he got three ribs broken.

Then, we wear moleskin trousers because any other sort of material chafes with the long hours in the saddle.

Then again, this station has its own store and we can get any sort of working clothes that we use while working here, and all employees get stuff at cost price.

The hats that are mostly worn are the broad-brimmed variety and I have one that ought to last for years.

Also, I've got mobs of shirts, seven, which are the correct hard-wearing drill and ought to last for a couple of years.

Sorry about those skins going astray. The emu and kangaroo skins can easily be replaced but I am doubtful about the fox — it was easily the best I have seen. However, I'll send another batch, which will be shot during winter, when the skin or rather fur is the thickest. I have just received a cheque for £4 10s for kangaroo skins, which I got at Rutherglen; they realised £5 and charged me 10 shillings for commission.

The drought up here is still continuing, in spite of the fact that there has been plenty of rain in Queensland and other states. Cattle are dying off in hundreds per day, and the loss to the Queensland National Pastoral Coy must be terrific. Unless we get rain soon there will be no cattle to go south this year, and they usually send 10 000–12 000.

In the event of cattle leaving here I shall try and go with them. It will probably be a 14 to 16 week trip and the pay is £4 per week and keep. I shall then either go straight back to the 'Lake' or go on one of the firm's southern Queensland stations

— they own 17 in all. Well, there is very little else to tell you, so I'll pack up, so cheerio.

Your loving son

LAKE NASH STATION

25–26 MARCH 1926

Dear Norman

I have several unanswered epistles of yours, not to mention the Xmas card, which arrived in March, so I s'pose I ought to take up my pen and write.

I might mention that until I received the last mail, during the two years I have been in this country I have received two letters from you. I said until the last mail because when that welcome day arrived I was literally swamped with correspondence from you. Two whole letters and a Christmas card.

I also received a couple of letters from Uncle Tom, who enclosed some photos of their latest domicile, which is quite an inspiring looking structure.

These letters, together with one or two others — a dozen or so from Australian friends plus Sunday parcels — comprised my mail.

I suppose you will be more or less interested in my latest address. As I have sent a brief description of the run, which by this time you have doubtless read, I will give you some idea of the head station.

From the distance it looks like a model township or a garden city, laid out in the form of a square several hundred yards across and painted white, it stands out in sharp contrast to the drab surrounding scenery. The manager's residence with its surrounding wealth of vegetation is the most striking building and forms one corner of the square. Between it and the next corner (which is the station store) come two very large buildings — the engineer's shop and the blacksmith's shop — easily distinguished by the motley collection of old cars, engines, bodies, wheels, buggies, buckboards, wagons, etc.

After the store, which I have already mentioned, comes the saddler shop, butcher shop, men's hut and dining hut, kitchen, jackeroos' dining room and jackeroos' sleeping quarters. Other odd buildings which are used for everything and anything complete the square.

The station is built on the Georgina River, which is the only water course that has water in it all the year round, even then it is usually a string of muddy waterholes and not very inviting. Just recently, however, it has been supplemented by the annual rains, but in this dry climate it will soon go down.

By the way, I never received those photos you promised to send me a couple of years ago. Did you ever send them? If you send me some photos, I'll send you some of branding; some of horsemen and some photos of them riding a 'dinkum' buck-jumper. A buckjumper, not a horse that just rears up and down, but a horse that will leap into the air and come down with its four feet together and with such force that the rider spits blood. Mind you I hope I'm not giving you the impression that horses are bad in the Territory — let me tell you there isn't a bad horse on the Lake.

There was one bad horse here but a good many years ago now (a Winchester 32.40 ended his career). Neither man nor devil could ride him, nor attempted to after he nearly killed the breaker. It was like this — The breaker had about 30 colts and fillies to break in that season with this particular horse amongst them. He got the head rope on him, threw him, sidelined him (sidelines are hobbles extending to the hind legs to prevent kicking), got the jewellery on (breaking-in tackle), head stall, etc.

However, after days of handling, the horse refused to quieten down like the others and above all refused to have a saddle on. He'd snort and squeal, kick, bite, strike, rear up but wouldn't have the saddle on. The breaker, however, had made up his mind the other way and one morning he roped and threw him and soon had his girth and surcingle buckled up. His offsider, a black fellow, was on the ropes and was ordered to let'er go, and as the horse was rising from the ground the breaker leapt on. The horsebreaker was quite a rider and it was generally supposed that anything that could buck him off 'could throw its own brand off'.

Well, the first buck loosened him, at the second he knew he was a goner, at the third — he was gone. The horse didn't stop at that.

As the man's body hit the ground, it rushed forward trampling and kicking at the inert form on the ground. Fortunately, the blackfellow was quickly on the scene and knocked the horse down with a waddy.

The man had a fractured leg, a broken collarbone, a broken arm, three ribs shoved in, and the lining of his stomach split — he had 500 miles to go to a doctor — and he lived.

It is impossible to describe the speed at which the horse bucked. An eyewitness said that from the time the man first hit the saddle to the time he hit the ground two seconds had elapsed — from my own personal experience of just lively horses, I can believe it.

This horse was generally considered bad.

Well, I will draw this rambling epistle to a close, hoping you will have a spare hour or two to unravel it. I shouldn't show all of this letter to Mum as she would have hysterics.

Your affectionate brother

STRATHFIELD
VIA MCKINLAY
NORTH-WEST QUEENSLAND

30 APRIL 1926

Dear Peg

I left Lake Nash and went into Dajarra... with no idea as to what I was going to do next. At ten o'clock on Tuesday (exactly 24 hours later) I was 200 miles away with a job, mustering and drafting bullocks.

In about nine weeks time I am going droving with 5000 cattle, going from here to Glenormiston Station to... Whatever my next address will be I haven't the faintest notion. I don't s'pose I'll have one as I shall probably be travelling all over Queensland with stock. I hope so anyway — it is best pay. On second thoughts, I think perhaps you had better write to this address as I can easily get it redirected.

I like it here better than Lake Nash as we work from the head station and are not camped out so much. Consequently, the food isn't so rough. We have a Japanese cook and he's jolly good.

As all the cattle are going away from here, they have to be separated, bullocks from breeders, fat cows, weaners and so on. This is done by camp drafting. All the cattle are mustered on a certain portion and are 'held' by the stockmen, while some 'gun' horseman (usually the head stockman) rides into the mob and runs out the beasts he wants one by one into the open, where they are held by other stockmen. We have some fearfully fast work. If a beast breaks out and tries to get to the other mob it has got to be fetched back. Also the 'cutter out' cuts the beast out of the mob and the stockman, who receives it to take it to the other mob (known as 'working on the face'), musn't let his beast get back to the mob it has just been cut out from. It's all very exciting work.

By the way there's an institution in Queensland known as the Golden Casket Art Union. It is in aid of Queensland hospitals with 813 prizes, ranging from £5000 to £5 and I took four tickets at 5 shillings each. I never thought any more about it 'till I picked up a fortnight old paper in Dajarra and on looking through the results, which happened to be in there, I saw I had drawn (climax at last) a fiver. True, my hopes had a few noughts in them, but it's better than nothing.

Well cheerio, your loving brother

C/- PO BOULIA
QUEENSLAND

15 NOVEMBER 1926

Dear everybody

I am taking this opportunity to write you a few lines as I don't expect another chance for a couple of months. So I hope you all have a jolly good Christmas and good trade and that.

I made out from Boulia a short time ago with my horses (just broken in) to catch a drover who wanted a man, but my horses were too fresh. My packhorse bucked my pack off twice and kicked it to pieces, a filly bucked over a stock yard and was away two days with the saddle on, and a chestnut colt jumped over a yard and went bush. I got them all together again (this was the first stage of the journey) and recounterlined my pack-saddle and patched it up. I started on the second stage of my journey. I intended getting an early start and go 75 miles that day. I got the early start, right enough, but I had only gone 15 miles when the packhorse started to buck and the pack-saddle went one way and the horses another, and by jingo they streaked. I gave them a 5 mile gallop, but had to give 'em best so now they are running on about 14 000 square miles of country, that is, if the border fence is up, if not they can get into every state bar Victoria. So all that remains of my turn-out is my saddle horse and a few straps. I've got a blackfellow out trying to pick up their tracks. But somehow I don't think he will as it is all sand hills and sand storms occur so often that I'm afraid their tracks will be covered. However, the sun's shining and there's plenty of work about.

I've just been offered a job droving, down Charleville way with a mob of a thousand fats. I haven't definitely decided yet, but if I do take it I don't suppose you will hear from me for a couple of months. I'll try to write. I'll get a fiver a week and keep out of it, so I don't care a hang how long it lasts. When it is finished I am going out into the Territory, Alexandria's way (a station bigger than Belgium). I remember you mentioning something about taking up a piece of ground for me. Don't do

anything until I am on the boat as it all rests in the lap of the
Gods and they haven't been smiling at all lately.

Well I must knock off now. I've got a horse to shoe and the
temperature is nearly a 100°F now and I want to get it done
before it's too hot — it's (the temperature) been going up to
115° and 117° this last day or so. It'll soon start to get hot!

Well love to everybody and Merry Xmas. C/- PO Boulia
will find me.

DURIE STATION,
BIRDSVILLE,
VIA WINDORAH, QUEENSLAND

1 FEBRUARY 1927

Dear Mum

It must be nearly two months since I wrote to you, so I s'pose
you will have been worrying about me, although there was no
necessity.

I had a rough trip with the bullocks and didn't go right
through with them. I was horse-tailer, that is, apart from doing
a watch at night, I had nothing to do with the cattle, having
complete charge of 40 odd head of horses. The cattle used to
travel five to 15 miles per day, and sometimes further according to what distance it was to water. They were terribly low in
condition and on three occasions there were distances of 30 and
35 miles between water, when a large number of the weakest
cattle died. My job was to take the horses from one camp to the
next and hobble them out. Then at sundown the cattle would
arrive and I would go and get the horses that were used for
night work only.

I would then take the first watch, this being the horse-
tailer's watch. Then in the morning I was called at 3.30 to go
out and get the stockmen's horses for the day. By the time I
arrived back the men had finished their breakfast, so they
saddled their horses and started the cattle on the road. Of
course when droving the cattle must not be driven (except on

long stages where there is no water) but fed along. After I had finished my breakfast I would unhobble the horses and put the pack saddles on and go to the next camp.

Sometimes the horses cleared out and then I had to track them up. On one occasion I tracked four horses 15 miles across the Bedourie sand hills after a sand storm.

Christmas day I spent on a dry stage coming from Monkira to Toonka and my Christmas dinner was tea, salt beef and damper. Well I will say goodbye. On second thoughts I think you had better write to me: C/- P.O. Boulia Queensland.

Goodbye, love to all, your loving son

BOULIA

10 APRIL 1927

Dear Mum

Just received your parcel and thanks very much for it. I have just come back to Boulia from Birdsville and found a lot of mail waiting for me, which I hadn't got owing to the Georgina River 'coming down'.

I am now with the same drover that I was with when I came from Strathfield to Glenormiston last year. We are at present waiting at Chatsworth Station and tomorrow we are taking delivery of 2000 head of mixed cattle, which we are taking to Coorabulka Station, consequently we are all hurry and bustle shoeing horses and one thing and another, so I haven't much time to write a long letter but I will do so as soon as I have the time to spare.

Thanks very much for all your birthday wishes. I spent my 21st birthday camped on Farrars Creek at a waterhole called Milkrie, mustering for Durie Station.

I don't know when I'm coming home but as soon as I get enough money. I will close now as I have a lot to do.

So goodbye, love to all, your loving son

BRUNETTE DOWNS
NORTHERN TERRITORY
VIA CAMOOWEAL
QUEENSLAND

1 JULY 1927

Dear Mum

Just a letter to give you an idea of my whereabouts. I am working at the above address, but I am pretty well fed up with it.

It is one of the largest cattle stations in the world and one of the lousiest, having an area of 12 000 square miles. They won't give a white a job if they can get a black. In the stock camp there are 11 of us and one other white man. There's 50 or 60 men employed and about eight or nine white men. They pay the lowest rate of wages of any station around here and the living is the hardest and roughest. However I can get work and I'm off as soon as it suits me to go.

You had better write to me C/- Post Office, Camooweal, Queensland.

The annual district race meeting was held the other week at a place called the Rankine. The Rankine races are a great event, being talked of for months beforehand. Everybody takes a great interest in racing as pretty nearly everybody is a racehorse owner.

Last year Brunette horses 'cleaned 'em up' — they got eight firsts (including the Rankine Gold Cup) and five seconds, consequently Brunette horses were the favourites. But the 5O5 brand only went to the front in one race. However, we got a third in the Gold Cup which is a mile and a half race with a large gold cup and 100 quid to boot. It was won this year by an Alroy Downs horse called One King, on whom I had a modest fiver at evens.

I wrote a piece of poetry on it, which I enclose. The following will serve as a reference list:

The Chrysler is the station speed car owned by a fellow named Hollingsworth. (There is a plain from the Buchanan

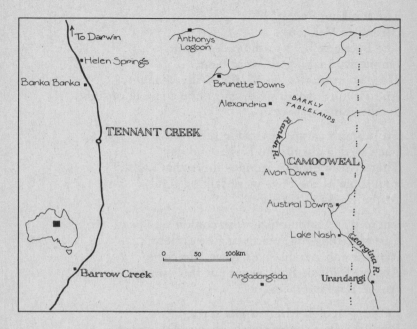

River to the Rankine River called the Rankine Plain, which is 28 miles across, without a tree of any description and is regarded as the local speedway. It is only a rough bush track and the Chrysler has the record with 21 minutes. One fellow nearly took it from the Chrysler but his tyre burst. His grave makes quite a decent halfway mark in the otherwise monotonous track.)

'Jimmy' is the cove who was training the Brunette horses.

As you will see in the second verse, some of the locally brewed 'fire water' made some of the boys 'fightable'.

You will be able to tell which names are horses.

The reference to Redlegs is a bit of a dig for the boss, as he gave the jockey, a halfcast boy, a few bob to 'pull' him.

Watson is the cove who had the 'grog shop'.

The Rankine Races 1927
(Brunette Version)
The Brunette boys to the races went,
On money making all were bent,
They went on the 'Ford', the Willys Knight,
And Hollingsworth's Chrysler, like a streak of light,
To the Rankine races.

To Jimmy's camp they made their way
Each with a cheque, so bright and gay,
There was a bit of a rumpus there that night
And some of the boys were talking fight,
At the Rankine races.

There was Minnetonka, who couldn't be beat,
Dissuade the grey, who was just as fleet,
Rainbar and Armbreaker were also certs,
And on Bodlam Boy they'd put their shirts,
At the Rankine races.

In the Bracelet, Minnetonka started,
From the first of their cash, they sadly parted,
On the chestnut Armbreaker, they had a win,
But agreed they were in for a very rough spin
At the Rankine races.

The Gold Cup was run on the following day,
With the brown horse third, they did not feel gay,
Armbreaker then had another start,
But all he broke, was the boss's heart,
At the Rankine races.

Rainbar couldn't run a decent last,
Dissuade and Sambo were just as fast,
Of Redlegs there seemed a bit of a mystery
But no one appeared to know the whole history
At the Rankine races.

Next day for home they made a start
From Watson's booth they had to part,

Each his own misfortune nursing
Inwardly and silently cursing
The Rankine races.

Well, well, I'll leave you to it. The water has 'chopped out' at
the Six Mile Waterhole and I have to go over with a mob of
boys to shift 'em tomorrow and it's getting late.

So love to all, your loving son
P.S. I am enclosing a block of four stamps printed to commem-
orate the opening of Canberra, so if any of the boys go in for
stamp collecting they can have 'em.

ANTHONY'S LAGOON
NORTHERN TERRITORY
VIA CAMOOWEAL, QUEENSLAND

19 SEPTEMBER 1927

Dear Peg

I don't hear much from you lately. Waffor you no more yabba
yabba? Mine tink it you coola phella longa meself ain't it?

It must be nearly six months since I heard from you. I dunno
whether you're in trouble, in love, in jail or what.

Although you see I've got a different address I'm still
working for Brunette, only at present I'm at one of the
outstations. There are three out-stations altogether, Anthony's
being closest to the head station (70 miles) Walhollow (120
miles) and Eva Downs (150 miles). Yep, she's a fair sized slab of
country this Brunette Downs, 12 000 square miles altogether.
No I haven't made a mistake with the noughts, twelve thousand's the figure.

When you go through the front gate you get to the front
door about 12 hours later (that is by car, by horse it's a day and a
half, yer pull up and camp at Crows Nest and hit the station
about midday next day). I s'pose I needn't come home now as
you've got Norman there, eh? — or at least not in such a blanky
hurry.

I'm thinking of taking up a block of country out here, in the Territory. What do'yr think of the idea. 100 square miles ought to be enough for a kick off. I've got plenty of horses, cattle are dirt cheap an' you can come and keep house for me!

If I had a bit of cash I'd be on it like a bird. I know where there's a mob of breeders going for £1 per head. Drought has broken the owner (like thousands of others). There'll be a big boom in cattle before long and gold won't buy 'em. People will be replacing the losses sustained in the drought and before long the meat export trade will be firmly established. Hitherto Australia has only been able to put frozen beef on the British market, but now they are experimenting with chilled beef, which has been unattainable owing to the producer being too far from the consumer. I dunno what you have to pay for beef over there but the producer here is lucky if he can average 1 pence per pound on his fats, and 3½ pence or 2 pence per lb would be wealth beyond the dreams of avarice to the poor cattle man. The Prime Minister says there's a silver lining, but nobody takes much notice of him. He's always making extravagant promises. Of course this is a bare outline. I could give you details with pages of figures showing costs of production because cattle is the one thing I know from A to Z and Z to A. But all that wouldn't interest you and you wouldn't understand it anyhow.

By the way I want to tell you people not to send me a parcel this year as owing to the uncertainty of my address, it might be six months after Xmas when I receive it. This is a rotten place I'm on now, but I want to hang on till the wet if I can as things are very slack everywhere owing to the drought in Queensland.

I heard today that there is a big railway strike in Queensland, although I don't know much about it. Camooweal is the nearest point in Queensland from here and incidentally the nearest town, and it is over 300 miles from here. The nearest railway is 500 miles and consequently news does not travel very swiftly.

Tell Mum that I'm sending her a birthday present. I sent for it some time ago, but it hasn't reached me yet and I s'pose this strike'll hold it up.

We are just coming to the end of the winter. It's been pretty mild. All I wore right through winter was boots, strides, shirt and lid, but no undershirt. One day it was 'bitterly' cold and I had to wear a cardigan and woollen coat nearly all day. The temperature was nearly down to 45 degrees. Gosh it was cold. Every time I think of England I get a sweat up shivering. I'm pretty hardy but I think a winter over there 'ud finish me off.

Oh well so long. Don't forget to drop a line to your affectionate brudder.
Tom

At Brunette Downs I was sent to an outstation seventy miles to the west called Anthony's Lagoon. I was to run the engine that in turn worked the pump of a bore. I was on my own. Bill Wilson, the manager knew I was not liking it and suggested when a new fellow applied for work that I take the opportunity to get out. He had four horses that belonged to a drover called Bill Crowson and he suggested I deliver them to him over at Wave Hill in early March. I twas October and there was no great hurry.

ANTHONY'S LAGOON
PO CAMOOWEAL
QUEENSLAND

OCTOBER 1927

Dear Mum

Just a short note to let you know I sent you a handbag the other day. I intended it for your birthday, but the blanky mails are so few and far between out this way that I don't suppose it will reach you much before Xmas. I have left Brunette and am now on my way westward travelling by horse. I have four with me. One pack horse and three riding horses. I left Anthony's

Lagoon three days ago and am only 70 miles from there now. Owing to the very dry state of the country just here I can't travel very fast, although from now on for the next 100 miles I shall have to go 25 miles per day as that is the distance the water is apart. When I get to Newcastle Waters I shall have done 170 miles, one of the longest leads in Australia. There is no store, station or any whiteman's abode, so consequently I've got to be very careful with my rations.

Don't worry if you don't get mail from me too often as along this track we have to rely on passers to take our mail into Queensland (360 miles from where I'm writing this) and post it. You can write to me at the above address as I shall drift back Queensland way as soon as it rains.

Wishing you all a Merry Xmas and a prosperous New Year.

Your loving son

I rode up to Banka Banka Homestead, a cattle station owned by Paddy and Jim Ambrose. After a couple of days I mentioned moving on, but the Ambroses pressed me to stay, not because of the odd jobs — but because they liked the company. It was suggested that I break in some horses. I hadn't done any horse breakinb before, although I had given a hand a few times, but I was confident I could do the job and I was anxious to get the experience. Paddy suggested that if I'd like to break in some colts I oculd have one for every four I broke in. I thought this was a good idea, since I didn't own the horses I was using and it suited the Ambroses because they couldn't afford to pay wages.

Banka Banka Station
Northern Territory
via Adelaide

13 December 1927

Dear Norman

It's a few weeks since I wrote to you (also a few since you wrote to me). So I'll give you a rough account of my doings of the last few weeks.

I left Anthony's Lagoon about the 19th of October with four horses and headed north-west for Newcastle Waters, a stage of 200 miles with water averaging every 25 miles. I got to Newcastle Waters a week later and camped there a few days to spell my horses, and then turned south, struck Powells Creek Telegraph Station, Renner Springs, Helen Springs (a small station of about 200 square miles owned by the Bohning family with whom I am very friendly) and finally Banka Banka Station where I took a job.

I have been here for some time now and am at present training a few racehorses for the Barrow Creek Races which, around here, is more important than the Derby, Melbourne Cup, and all other races put together.

I don't know whether I shall go to it yet as it is 200 miles to Barrow Creek and the country is very bad for about 100 miles between here and there. The whole question rests with me as I am the trainer. If I say yes then yes it is. I am very keen on going but I'm not going to murder horses doing it. If I go I shall ride the horses myself and if things go well I shall have hopes of winning a few races. I've got one very nice black colt in hand and he gallops very well for me. He's not much good at anything under a mile as it takes about 6 furlongs to warm him and, by the Seven Holy Cities, after he's gone 7 or 8 furlongs he's laying down to it. The only thing that gets the breeze up me is he's a devil at the barrier and I'm frightened he'll get left at the post. Anyhow, we'll see.

If I take the Banka horses and go to the races, which are on the 26th and 27th of this month, and it's pretty well a cert that

I'll have a few mounts, it will be the first Xmas since I've been in Australia that I haven't been working and I'm going to have a good time you can bet your life on that. I s'pose you've heard of community singing? — well, this is community boozing! The club buys the booze and everybody drinks it, and nothing to pay! The nominations went in today and I've got horses nominated for the Maiden Plate, Barrow Creek Handicap, Weight for Age, Flying Handicap and the Ladies Bracelet. If I don't scratch any I hope to land a few races out of it.

Yours etc., love to all and sundry
P.S. After Xmas I have 50 or 60 head of colts to break in and after that expect to go west with a mob (200) of Banka horses, which are sold to Victoria River Downs, the largest cattle station in the world (12 000 square miles) owned by Bovril. So you can call Banka my address. I haven't received any mail since I left Anthony's Lagoon and shall not do so until after Xmas, so excuse me if there are letters that I ought to have answered and haven't.

A fellow called Alec Moray offered me a job as head stockman at Wave Hill. Being head stockman of the most famous station in the Australian Pastoral division of Vesteys gave me a lot of satisfaction. I left my horses at Banka Bank with the Ambroses and left for Wave Hill.

At this time the Northern Territory was divided into two regions each with its own administrator. Above the 20th parallel was called North Australia, below it was Central Australia.

WAVE HILL STATION
NORTH AUSTRALIA

29 SEPTEMBER 1928

Dear Mum

Have just received your letter or rather, I should say, I received it a week or so ago but owing to circumstances was unable to answer it.

I am head stockman of Number One camp on Wave Hill. I have been here about two and a half months, but most of the time have been off the run over at Mt Sanford, an outstation of Victoria River Downs. I have been getting Wave Hill cattle that have strayed through the boundary, I got about 300 all told.

I am camped at a bore at present with 1500 head of bullocks, which I'm looking after until it rains, when all the water holes will be filled. The rains aren't due yet and I expect to be camped here for a month or so. Tomorrow I am splitting the camp up and sending half the boys to another bore, where there is about 1200 bullocks watering, about 12 miles from here.

I don't know how it is you never received a letter from me for about six months as I write oftener than that. I s'pose they must have gone astray, anyhow if it occurs again you've no need to worry like that, just write to my last address and the mail is always forwarded. Of course I know a lot of mail doesn't reach me as it gets washed away in floods and that sort of thing.

My love to all and sundry, your loving son

I left Wave Hill with some regret. I'd had a good camp to run, the stockmen were very good, it was beautiful country and fairly easy to work. But there was too much friction between the manager and myself. I was all set to do some breaking at Banka Banka when I was offered a job with the Overland Telegraph as a linesman.

TENNANT CREEK
NORTH AUSTRALIA

15 DECEMBER 1928

Dear Mum

The wet season is now over two months overdue, so I have decided to give the desert trip the go by. It is certainly impossible to go out there now as there has been no rain for over 18 months.

I have decided to settle here for a few weeks, so have taken a job as linesman. Tennant Creek is a telegraph station on the overland telegraph line. There are two of us (that is, whites) here. An operator named Woodroffe and myself.

I have 120 miles of telegraph line to keep in order, that is, repair any breaks in the wires 60 miles south and 60 miles north. However, breaks very rarely occur and my time is mostly occupied in branding and looking after the 300 to 400 head of cattle, which keep us in beef, and about 200 head of horses.

There is a fairly large encampment of blacks here, from where we draw our working staff.

Our nearest neighbours are to the north, Banka Banka, 60 or 70 miles, and to the south, Barrow Creek, 270 miles. Barrow Creek is another telegraph station similar to here and Banka is a station where I was breaking-in last year. I know all this country fairly well and pretty well everybody knows me. As I daresay, you will remember I was down at 'The Barrow' last Xmas with race horses.

We are right in the big central desert, which stretches for over 1000 miles to the west and about 700 to the south and east. In the desert there is a tribe of blacks called the Walamullas, who are a continual source of annoyance. They come into these stations pilfering and fighting with the tribes already here and elsewhere. They have killed five whites at Barrow Creek, all told, having on one occasion wiped out the telegraph station.

A month ago they speared an old chap named Fred Brooks and chopped another chap about called Nugget Morton.

Of course, us chaps in these telegraph stations are quite safe as the blacks have more sense than to interfere with the government property, and also, these are stone buildings built in the form of a fort, so you needn't worry about me getting hurt.

Well there is no news of any interest to you, so will close.

Love to all, your loving son

I decided life as a linesman was not for me. Sometime later with my horses and gear I made my way to Bullita Station, one of five cattle stations owned by the Duracks. The manager of the station, Tom Lawson needed a stockman and two days later I was out mustering. Bullita was not the easiest place to muster it was 2000 miles of rough and scrubby country.

BULLITA STATION
KATHERINE
NORTH AUSTRALIA

10 JUNE 1929

Dear Mum

Since writing to you last quite a lot of things have happened.

As I told you in my last letter I was only here for the bullock muster, however, an accident happened and sort of threw things out of gear.

We had been out on the run mustering for nearly a month and were doing our last day's work in that section. We had mustered the country around a yard called Bob's Yard and yarded the cattle about sundown. During the night a lot of cattle got out of the yard as it was very old and fairly rotten, so we decided to brand the cleanskins and watch the bullocks the following night and we reckoned to get into the station the next day as it was only 15 miles. However, we started branding. The branding is done as follows:

In the plant there is always a horse called the bronco horse, who does nothing but work in a branding or bronco yard. (In this case, the bronco horse was a chestnut mare and she was saddled up in the morning and a long greenhide rope attached to the saddle. I rode her at first — I rode into the cattle and started catching or lassoing the calves that were to be branded.) A calf is caught and dragged up to what is called a bronco ramp, then it is leg roped and thrown and then branded.

After branding about 25 calves, the manager called me to change over — he went 'catching' and I worked on the ground. We branded about ten more, but there was one big white cleanskin cow that had been missed in many previous musters. Lawson, the manager, caught her and dragged her up to the ramp. As he was holding her for us to legrope her, she gave two quick successive plunges. The first one threw the bronco mare off her balance and, before she could recover, the cow plunged again, and the horse and rider, in a cloud of dust, crashed to the ground. Lawson lay still, but the horse struggled to its feet and, before we could drag him away, the horse crashed again on top of him. I slashed the rope and then freed the horse which could then get up and we got him away to the shade.

I thought at first he was dead and I had the breeze up properly as I was on my own with a mob of blacks for stockmen. However, after a while he came to but I could see he was badly hurt. Anyhow, I went over to a drover, who happened to be going through, to get some Bovril for him. I was away about an hour as it was some way over, and when I came back he (Lawson) had the camp packed up and was on his horse starting into the station. He seemed very dazed and wasn't too sure of himself, however, he was boss, so it wasn't much good me arguing.

We had gone about a mile and I suddenly discovered that our dog was missing, so I lapped back for it and found it and started back. However, I hadn't gone too far when I discovered that the tracks of the cattle were not on the pad, so I started circling to try and pick them up. I was considerably puzzled as there was only the one road to the station. However, by this time it was dark, so I rode over to where I knew a drover was camped, and I camped with him that night and rode into the station in the morning.

About sundown the same day, Lawson got in with the cattle and, of course, the blacks. Where they had been to, Heaven only knows.

I could see at once that Lawson's fall had affected his brain. The cook and I put him to bed. The next morning he was no better and was drinking kerosene and acting generally like a harmless lunatic.

I could see the way things were, so about midday, without waiting for dinner, I saddled up a horse and started into what we call the 'Depot', 45 miles distant. This is a store and a police station on the Victoria River, where a lugger comes about every two months in the winter and not at all in the summer. I got into the police station about 9 p.m. and the policeman happened to be in for once, and not out hunting blacks.

He told me that M. P. Durack, one of the owners of the station, had left a few hours previously by car and intended camping at Auvergne Station, one of his properties, and was leaving there after breakfast the next morning. There was no car in the Depot, so I changed my horse and rode straight on to Auvergne. By travelling all night I reckoned to make Auvergne by day break. Anyhow, I got in about sunrise and I must say those two horses put up a good lap. One did 45 miles without pulling up and the other did 35 miles — as game as fighting cocks.

The car came straight back to Bullita. Durack took Lawson into Wyndham, to the nearest doctor, about 200 miles from here. The doctor says Lawson may get right but not inside six months — he does not seem very optimistic. It's a terrible thing when a man's reason goes. Anyhow, in the meantime, I am managing Bullita.

It is nothing great as jobs go. The country is reckoned to be amongst the roughest in the north and that's going some. The cattle are wild as Marchhares and machine guns and aeroplanes are needed to muster the horses. However, I'm getting £250 per annum and keep, so I s'pose it's something to be earning a crust.

I am going for my life mustering and branding. I branded 70 calves today, so am pretty tired.

I will say goodbye now. Write and let me have all the news.

Love to all, your loving son

When Lawson eventually recovered I was happily on my way again. I had my mind set on doing some horse breaking and I headed west for Hall's Creek in Western Australia.

WATERLOO STATION
1930

... I am back working for Vesteys again. That is the same company that owns Wave Hill. I started at Ord River Station, which is just outside the Territory in Western Australia, but got a transfer to Waterloo to break in horses.

I have 20 head of fillies to break in and they are paying £1 5s per head and keep. It is not extra good as horse breaking goes, but I can knock about £7 10s per week out of it, which is not too bad. I could get a good run out of it, say 80 to 100 colts.

When I have finished here, they may send me to Limbunya Station to break in, but I don't know for sure. They may put me as head stockman somewhere. I have been doing fairly well this last couple of years and at the end of this year another chap and myself are going over to inspect a small cattle property, which is under offer to us. Nothing is definite yet and I will let you know more about it later.

I would like to get in somewhere as there is every indication of the cattle market booming, following the long period of drought in Queensland. Large numbers of large stations have been wiped right out and this represents an enormous shortage of cattle. Three stations in the Boulia district used to send 6000 bullocks into the meat works every year, and this, with many others, went under.

I received your letter last mail saying you were sending me a pair of binoculars. I s'pose they will come along later. The reason I never mentioned anything was because I thought that due to the way you are situated, it would be better to save the money. I always have 100 or so, but this fluctuates as I am always buying and selling horses, but I never go short of anything.

[Ed. Tom turned 24 in February 1930.]

Love to all, your loving son

I finished at Limbunya Station in September with a pocket full of cheques. I decided to leave my horses and gear at Limbunya and head for Darwin. I got through to Pine Creek where I caught the train to Darwin. It was still another three months until the wet season. I was just getting bored with Darwin when I was asked to do some breaking on Burnside Station at Brocks Creek and then to go on to Mt Litchfield Station an outstation of Burnside, 70 miles to the west.

C/- RUNDLE & CO
KATHERINE
NORTH AUSTRALIA

1 DECEMBER 1930

Dear Mum

Have just got a few photos of myself, so thought I would send them along. They are not good photos of me as they make me appear about twice my age.

They were taken at Litchfield, an outstation of Burnside, where I was colt breaking. There is one of me riding a bucking filly called Chance, but it is very difficult to take a photo of a buckjumper as it is here, there and everywhere. She (Chance) bucked right out of the picture at the critical moment and, anyhow, the photographer waited too long, so by the time he 'snapped' she had just finished bucking — but she could buck pretty. Also there is a photo of a brown colt in tackling — a very decent photo — the brand and running number can be clearly seen. This colt also had a good idea of bucking, although the general run of them were pretty good.

I also broke some mules in here. It was my first experience with breaking them, 'tho I have worked them a good bit as I own three myself, and all the pack work is done with mules in this country.

I will try to send you some local papers, which may interest you. When you see and read them, it will be difficult to realise it is the only paper in a state many times larger than England.

The wet has just set in now and everything on wheels is hung up. However, the good old packhorse 'comes to light' when everything else fails — ploughing across black soil plains and swimming rivers — slow but sure.

There is nothing to write about, so will close. It is Norman's birthday today, so many happy returns to him.

Much love, your loving son

*I had become friendly with Harry Hardy, the buffalo shooter at Brocks
Creek and he asked me if I'd like to take a job buffalo shooting. I
didn't hesitate, I took the job. The shooting would start about May,
after the worst of the wet season. My horses and gear were at
Limbunya and there were a lot of rivers that would have to be swum
to get there to collect them. I had four months to get there and back —
a thousand miles.*

C/- RUNDLE & CO
KATHERINE
NORTH AUSTRALIA

15 MAY 1931

Dear Len

It isn't too often that I write to you, but I suppose you get all the
news from Mum.

Winter is starting here, altho' the temperature was 85°F in the
shade today. But of course, you will see by your map that we are
many hundreds of miles north of the tropic of Capricorn and are
therefore well in the tropics. I am at present at a place called
Burrundie. You won't see this marked on the map but it is 124 miles
south of Darwin. Darwin is where all the airmen first land on
Australian soil. Miss Amy Johnson arrived there, this time last year.

I have most of my horses here with me. I also have a couple
of mules, altho' I only have one with me. These are extremely
hardy animals and are generally used for carrying packs. They
have good tough hides and do not chafe carrying a pack like a
horse does. Also, they are very hard in the feet and do not need
to be shod and they can carry terrific loads (compared to a
horse) with ease. Most men don't like them and won't have
them owing to their treacherous nature. They are generally
scoundrels and have to be watched, but provided one
remembers that a mule is a mule and throws no chances away,
there should be no trouble. I swopped a very ordinary horse for
a very good mule, and the cove I got him off told me he had
only seen one good mule and he was dead!

Well Len, I will have to knock off now. Hope you are getting on all right at school.

Your loving brother

Hardy's place was called Annaburroo, from the native word for buffalo, annaburra. We started shooting at his buffalo camp on the Mary River. Buffalo were everywhere. Unfortunately Harry couldn't keep me on. It was bad news because I was enjoying myself enormously. When I left I knew what I was going to do. As soon as I could I was going buffalo shooting.

C/- RUNDLE & CO
KATHERINE
NORTH AUSTRALIA
29 JUNE 1931

Dear Peg

Received your wedding cake, also books, and will send you a wedding present when I am financial. Things are pretty bad here just now, what with the depression and one thing and another.

I have just come in from the Mary River where I have been buffalo shooting and am off to Central Australia to break in a mob of colts.

I was head stockman on Wave Hill (one of the biggest stations in the world) in 1928, managing Bullita in 1929 and have been horse breaking for Vesteys ever since. It is about the best paid game on a station. I was making £10 a week on Burnside last year and was doing quite well until the depression set in. All the stations have cut excess with the result that there's a lot of good men riding about the country. I have a couple of gallopers and hoped to sell them, but I couldn't do this without sacrificing them, but this I refuse to do. They are a couple of good, honest colts of the St Anton line and one is very fast for half a mile and worth hanging on to. However, I don't suppose this will interest you much.

Here are some items that may interest Bill. Four year old bullocks are selling for 35 shillings per head on the station or run. However, this is, of course 1000 miles from the rail head (Alice Springs) and another 600 or 700 miles to Adelaide (the nearest market).

These bullocks would probably dress about 600 to 700 pounds as they have not matured at that age in this country. Of course, it doesn't pay to grow cattle at that price. Wyndham meat works are paying 18 shillings 6 pence per 100 pounds for prime beef, 7 shillings 6 pence for second grade and 4 shillings 6 pence for third. Of course, nobody can land prime beef as they have too far to drive them.

Victoria River Downs, the property of Bovril Ltd, used to send 12 000 bullocks in every year. In mobs of 750, they had over 400 miles to walk and towards the end of the season there was no grass because it was cleaned out by previous mobs, so they sometimes had to go 40 miles without a drink.

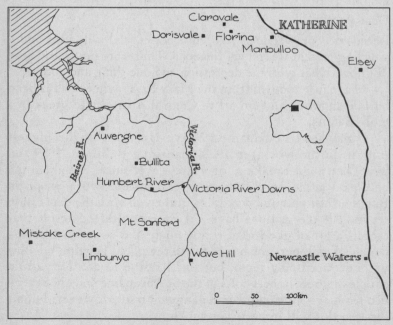

In 1930, I took 500 bullocks in for Duracks and had a 46 mile dry stage, and fats cut up considerably on that stage. I had to 'stand 'em up' for a day and a night, which doesn't improve fats. Of course, 46 miles is not considered a long dry stage here. In 1928, when running the camp on Wave Hill, I took delivery of 1250 Sturts Creek bullocks — they had done 76 miles without a drink two days previously — the drover only delivered three short, which was pretty good. But these bullocks were not fats but were what we call stores, and so they have to put a season in on a fattening property.

Well, we are in the middle of winter here and it's devilish hot; one just lies on top of the blankets and sweats until about 1 am and then a blanket may be needed. I've never seen weather like it. Generally, we get a sweat up shivering until about 9 a.m. at this time of the year.

Must close now as I have a horse to shoe, and must hop into him while I've got my second wind.

Love and all that

C/- RUNDLE & CO
KATHERINE
NORTH AUSTRALIA

30 JUNE 1931

Dear Mum

Have just received your letter of April 28th. There is nothing much you could send me as really I do not need for anything. I dare say you got my letter acknowledging the binoculars before this one. There is no sign of the stereoscope from Uncle Tom. I think it must have gone astray and would advise him to make enquiries for it. A thermos flask would not be of any use here as it would never stand the knocking about on packhorses and one always has time to boil the billy.

This life doesn't affect my health — I'm pretty tough — all us fellows get hardened to this sort of life. It's quite common for me to go without a midday meal. In fact, when I'm

52   RIDING THE WILDMAN PLAINS

THURSDAY, APRIL 2, 1931.

N.S.W. AND FEDERAL GOVT. TROUBLE

FEDERAL GOVT. TO PAY N.S.W. DEBT

SPLIT IN LABOR PARTY

FEDERAL PARTY'S ULTIM-ATUM

Sydney, Tuesday.

A special meeting of the Federal Cabinet yesterday deputed Scullin and Thodore to deal with the position in the New South Wales default in British interest payments. It is understood the Ministry recognised the moral if not the legal obligation to meet the London commitment of New South Wales by to-morrow. It is considered likely the Commonwealth will meet the position. They are now investigating the process by which it can be recovered from the state under the financial agreement.

With the object of smashing the Lang control of the State Labor Party the Federal conference has decided to establish a new Labor Party in New South Wales. An ultimatum has been served on all electorate councils and Labor Leagues and affiliated unions that they must pledge allegiance to the Federal Labor Party by April 30, otherwise they will be expelled.

The Federal Conference carried a motion repudiating the Lang Plan. If Lang fails to agree and abide by the Federal Party constitution he will be automatically placed outside the movement.

Brisbane, Tuesday.

The Queensland Premier has suggested to Victoria, South Australia, West Australia, and Tasmania, that each should petition the Governor of New South Wales to dissolve the Parliament of that State in view of Lang's default in interest payments.

Melbourne, Tuesday.

A ten per cent cut in award rates for over forty unions was granted by the Full Arbitration Court yesterday afternoon. The reductions applied from midnight last night. The court refused to redu. the

the new party will probably be supported by funds voted by Labor Party Branches in other States and donations from Labor supporters dissatisfied with the Lang rule.

The Lang Cabinet has decided to appoint a committee to fix the price of bread, pollard, wheatmeal, and other wheat by-products.

Canberra, Wednesday.

Statements that he might relinquish the Senate seat and contest Ballarat in the House of Representatives were refuted by Senator Barnes.

Mr. Fenton declared that he has no intention of retiring from politics, especially in view of the present situation.

Sydney, Wednesday.

Payment was made by the Commonwealth Government yesterday of £725,251 interest due by New South Wales Govt. to British bondholders. The Federal Government will take action at the earliest possible date for the recovery of the sum from the State. Prompt action by the Scullin Cabinet brought many congratulatory cable messages to the Prime Minister from all quarters. Mr. Brennan, attorney-general, with the co-operation of the Federal Crown Law Department, is preparing for the necessary recovery proceedings.

AUSTRALIAN ON FLIGHT HOME

BROADBENT LEAVES LONDON

London, Tuesday.

H. F. Broadbent, aged twenty, of Sydney, left England at six o'clock on Sunday morning on a solo flight to Australia. He is the first Australian trained airman to attempt the journey. He made a lonely and unobtrusive departure, taking off without any preliminary ascent. He expects to do five hundred miles daily, flying via Nuremberg, Budapest, Sofia, Aleppo, Bagdad, thence the usual course across India to Singapore. He planned to reach the Australian Coast at Wyndham, flying south to Perth, thence east Adelaide, Melbourne

THE ADVENTURER

The versatility of Tim McCoy will be demonstrated next Tuesday night at the Don Cinema. Tim McCoy features in the Metro Goldwyn Mayer picture "The Adventurer."

The story revolves round the revenue obtained from the gold mines of the South American Republic of Costa Ora, which Jim McClellan manages. Rafael el Tornado, an ambitious matador, accuses the President of the Republic of virtually handing over the mines to a foreign power, and incites the fickle populace to rebellion. He then imprisons the President and threatens to have him shot unless Dolores, his beautiful daughter, consents to be his wife.—The story of Jim McClellan's blood-tingling adventure in deposing the interloper, Tornado, and ultimatley rescuing the girl, is strikingly told.

A particularly good cast appears in this vigorous and stirring production. McCoy has the role of Jim McClellan, and carries it off most admirably. Beautiful Dorothy Sebastian plays Dolores de Silva, and makes most of the Spanish atmosphere. Included among the other well-known players, Charles Delaney as Barney, Jim McClellan's assistant, is worthy of praise.

This picture will appeal greatly to lovers of actionful, dashing and romantic stories.

The supporting picture is a story of the human side of the famous Artists Colony of Paris, featuring Vera Reynolds. Title of picture, "The Divine Sinner." Gazette and comedy. For your reservations phone two seven (Don Pictures).

MURDER AND SUICIDE

DAUGHTER'S SHOCKING DISCOVERY

Brisbane, Wednesday

A woman stabbed in se places about the neck and chest her brother-in-law with his t cut were found in a hous Drayton Street, Dalby. They Ida Mary Rook, r.3. wife travelling with packs on my own, I usually don't bother to 'pull up' in the middle of the day unless it is exceptionally hot, and then one has to for the sake of the horses.

As I told you in a previous letter, I received a letter from Peg and Hilda but no word from Norman. When I received your letter last year telling me of Norman's engagement I wired congrats. and also wrote, but I have not received any reply — in fact I don't even know his wife's name. I replied to Peg by this mail and promised to send her a wedding present when I am more financial. I suppose that is what she wrote for. Anyhow, I won't begrudge for a tenner when I have it to spare.

Just at present things are in a shocking state and all wages are being drastically cut — Australia as a working man's paradise has passed. For some years there will be very little over a bare existence.

I can get horse breaking and go from one station to another, and I shall stick to it for as long as I can as it is the best paid game. The only thing bad about it is the time lost and expense incurred going from one station to another. Last year I had to go from Limbunya to Burnside, a distance of 400 miles by road and over 1100 by rail. This is the furthest I have travelled in one hop. I left my horses and packs at Limbunya (it being the dry season) and came in by car, but I had to go back by packhorse (with the mail man) to get my horses as the wet had set in.

I am writing from a place called Adelaide River, where I am putting in a few days waiting for word regarding a mob of colts to be broken in at a station called Nutwood Downs. I will probably break in again at Burnside this year, but they do not get theirs broken until later on and if I get the Nutwood colts that would suit me very well. The stations are only a couple of hundred miles distant; Burnside is on the railway line and Nutwood is fairly handy.

I am expecting a letter from you again today as the southern mail gets in today.

Will close with fondest love, your loving son

My next encounter with buffalo shooting was for a buffalo shooter
called George Hunter. I took over running his camp after selling him
some horses. We did a deal based on a 50/50 split of the profits.

ADELAIDE RIVER

DECEMBER 1931

Dear Mum

... I have just spent a very enjoyable Christmas with a good
bush family — a chap named Hazel Gaden, a buffalo shooter
who shoots at Marrakia. I am camped at a place called Adelaide
River and am 'hitting the breeze' tomorrow morning for
Woolner, where I will probably be buffalo shooting next year.
Woolner is right down on the coast and we have a wet season
camp right on the beach.

If we are buffalo shooting next year we want to get a load
(250) of hides into Darwin by April. To do this, I have to go
down straight away as the wet season is right on us and I have a
number of swamps and rivers to cross, which are dry now but
will run rapidly as soon as the heavy wet sets in. If they flood, I
won't be able to get through until about May or June. Actually,
the wet is about finished in March.

I have about three months to put in. When I leave Adelaide
River tomorrow morning I am leaving the last link with
civilization. Tomorrow I will camp on the Margaret River and
shall strike Marrakia Station the following night, where I will
see the last white man for three months. The next night I shall
camp at Wild Boar Lagoon and Lake Finnis the next night. The
following day I shall reach Cape Hotham, my destination.
George Hunter has gone to Brisbane for the wet and won't be
back until March, so until I get down to the coast, there will be
nobody but blacks down there.

Love to all

1932

1 JANUARY 1932 — FRIDAY
Arrived back at Cape Hotham with horses lost from last
year's shooting camp.

11 JANUARY 1932 — MONDAY
Preparing for trip into Darwin for rations. I will have to go
as far as Adelaide River with horses, cross by canoe, walk to
Koolpinyah Station and borrow horses to continue journey.

12 JANUARY 1932 — TUESDAY
To Old Man Rock with packs. Unpacked and sent horses
back to camp.

19 JANUARY 1932 — TUESDAY
Darwin. Saw Kingsford Smith arrive from England with
mail. Left Darwin and camped Rapid Creek.

20 JANUARY 1932 — WEDNESDAY
Left Rapid Creek and camped Mu Wah Lagoon, where
Herberts are repairing yard.

22 JANUARY 1932 — FRIDAY
Left for river, crossed and walked onto camp; arrived about
3.00 a.m.

24 JANUARY 1932 — SUNDAY
Shot a shark.

8 FEBRUARY 1932 — MONDAY
Shot an alligator.
To avoid confusion the term alligator was used to describe saltwater crocodiles and the term crocodile described the less dangerous smaller freshwater crocodiles.

9 FEBRUARY 1932 — TUESDAY
Decidedly fed up with living here on my own with natives.
Left for Koolpinyah as per invitation.

28 FEBRUARY 1932 — SUNDAY
My 26th birthday.

15 MARCH 1932 — TUESDAY
Left Koolpinyah with Evan Herbert for Darwin by
packhorse. Raining like H–L. Camped 20 Mile.

19 MARCH 1932 — SATURDAY
Darwin. Air force squadron in from Sydney.

20 MARCH 1932 — SUNDAY
More planes. Met all the flying men. Wild and woolly time.

21 MARCH 1932 — MONDAY
Picnic with flying mob and some local lads. More wildness
and wool.

22 MARCH 1932 — TUESDAY
Fräulein from Berlin and seaplanes from home.
This was the first women to fly alone to Australia from Europe. She flew a Klemm Swallow aeroplane.

23 MARCH 1932 — WEDNESDAY
Left by train for 20 Mile. Evan Herbert met me with
buckboard and onto Koolpinyah.

24 MARCH 1932 — THURSDAY
Crossed river in broken derelict canoe by means of tarpaulin wrapped around it. Arrived Cape Hotham midday.

22 APRIL 1932 — FRIDAY
Started to Lake Finnis. After wet season the plains are all lakes. Arrived at Lake Finnis with everything thoroughly wet, including matches.

23 APRIL 1932 — SATURDAY
Buffalo camp.

29 JUNE 1932 — WEDNESDAY
Stan Brown left for Pine Creek with plant. Horses bolted with dray and smashed it up. The only parts left intact are the wheels and axle.

30 JUNE 1932 — THURSDAY
Repairing dray.

4 JULY 1932 — MONDAY
Finished dray. Mustered horses this morning in readiness for another start.

5 JULY 1932 — TUESDAY
Started for Pine Creek and camped Daly River.

6 JULY 1932 — WEDNESDAY
Horses away. Unable to leave until after dinner. Crossing very bad — Bamboo Grass 10 feet high. Crossed river and camped Maori Jack's peanut farm.

13 JULY 1932 — WEDNESDAY
Pine Creek. Rounding up horses all day. As soon as I find one I lose another. Have a dray and 16 horses, half of them unbroken. Too much for one man. Must get some boys.

14 JULY 1932 — THURSDAY
Pine Creek. Jack Sagabiel joined my camp.

19 JULY 1932 — TUESDAY
Bought four horses, a riding saddle and two packs. Jack repairing riding saddle. Self wedging dray wheel.

20 JULY 1932 — WEDNESDAY
Repaired harness. Put tailboard in dray. Wrote up six months mail.

21 JULY 1932 — THURSDAY
Left Pine Creek and went a mile and camped. Jack Sagabiel left for Katherine to get some more horses for me.

23 JULY 1932 — SATURDAY
Long day today. Arrived Mary River at dark and camped. Put unbroken horses across river and let them go.

24 JULY 1932 — SUNDAY
Crossed river at sunrise. Heavy pull from river bed. Arrived Goodparla Station.

C/- H. J. FOSTER
SOLICITOR
DARWIN NT

25 JULY 1932

Dear Mum

This is the last letter you will receive from me for some time to come. I am starting out for my country the day after tomorrow with 21 horses, a dray and my buffalo boys.

As I think I told you in my last letter, I required some more capital owing to the fact that I did not get paid by Hunter. I have taken Foster in on halves until 1 May 1936, so I don't expect to make a great deal this year. I have a few debts to settle, after which I expect to have about £50, but I should get a flying start next year.

I now hold 100 square miles of country on the West Alligator River — not a very big holding but I expect to extend it to 300 miles next year. There are a good few buffalo running about there and I expect to get about 400 hides this year. I have signed the agents up to take 200 at 4½ pence per pound and we expect to clear £200. The remaining 200 hides we may not be able to get in to Darwin this season as the wet will be on about November and I won't be shooting until August, and it will take me until nearly then to get my contract number. If I can't get them in then I will poison them and stack them until after the wet.

It's an awful struggle getting started and the expense is terrifying. I have sent for about three tons of salt by lugger and over half a ton of rations, and it's costing £11 15s per ton for freight alone. However, once I get out there and get established I will be right — but I've had a lot of reverses.

I had a letter and photo from Auntie Minnie and I am answering it tonight. I don't know whether I owe Don or Len a letter; I probably do as I'm a haphazard correspondent. I'll have to send them a promise. I would like to write to Peg but have lost her address and can't for the life of me remember it.

I will close now and if I get a chance to get a letter in by native or some other way, I will write to you and let you know how I am faring.

Love to all, your loving son

25 JULY 1932 — MONDAY
Dray horses tired, so having a day's spell. Handled three unbroken colts. One got away with rope and halter on. Paddy tracked it till dark and reported that by the look of its tracks it was still galloping.

26 JULY 1932 — TUESDAY
Sent Paddy off at day break to pick up colt's tracks. Self started on with plant. Paddy caught me up but no colt. Got

too much of a start. Paddy says "Galloping all way
sundown". Camped at South Alligator River.

27 JULY 1932 — WEDNESDAY
Bad river crossing — had to unload dray to pull it out of
river. Dray horses started to tire, camped Barramundi Creek.

28 JULY 1932 — THURSDAY
Bad day, today. Unbroken colts cleared out last night. Bad
country — had to cut my way through. Followed
Barramundi Creek down — a lot of heavy sand. Camped
about 10 miles down creek. Bad camp. Horse feed very poor.

29 JULY 1932 — FRIDAY
Another bad day. No water for horses today. Had to unyoke
horses and leave dray in the bush and go onto Jim Jim for
water. Arrived Jim Jim Crossing at dark and camped.

30 JULY 1932 — SATURDAY
Gave dray horses a day's spell. Self and Paddy rode all day
looking for buffalo. Saw one bull. No shooting. Saw many
blackfellow tracks.

1 AUGUST 1932 — MONDAY
Dray horses done in as got bogged in a swamp. Unloaded
dray but no good. Bogged to the axle. Abandoned dray and
went on with packs. Return for dray when swamp dries.

2 AUGUST 1932 — TUESDAY
Arrived Kapalga at last, to find my rations and salt. Rations
tampered with, probably blacks. Gaden taken 400 .303
bullets. Put in half a day handling colts and packing salt into
packbags. Took 600 pounds of salt.

3 AUGUST 1932 — WEDNESDAY
Tried to get early start, but no good. Horses didn't get in
until midday. Camped second Flying Fox Crossing.

4 AUGUST 1932 — THURSDAY
Arrived at a fairly large creek, which has no name and is not
marked on any map. Plenty of water so decided to make a
camp here. Large numbers of buffalo tracks here. Start
shooting tomorrow.

5 AUGUST 1932 — FRIDAY
Shot one bull and one cow. Very poor start — will have to
improve. Tried out several horses for shooting and lost
several buffalo as a consequence. Very thick timber here —
bad for galloping.

6 AUGUST 1932 — SATURDAY
Two bulls — the heaviest hides I have ever seen. It was with
the greatest difficulty that two boys and myself lifted them
onto the horses.

8 AUGUST 1932 — 'BLACK' MONDAY
Wounded bull jammed me in the scrub and ripped Cracker,
letting his entrails out. Threw him and sewed him up. All I
had to operate with was a skinning knife and string from a
flour bag. He has a chance to pull through.

9 AUGUST 1932 — TUESDAY
Must shift to a better camp as soon as I get my dray out of
the swamp.

10 AUGUST 1932 — WEDNESDAY
Nothing today. Flying Fox getting shot out. Cracker turned
up at the camp this morning, miles from where he was
horned. I think he will live, although very sick at present.
Shot a wild pig — thousands of them here.

11 AUGUST 1932 — THURSDAY
Four bulls, a record for this camp. Must go to Kapalga for
more salt tomorrow and shift camp when I return.

12 AUGUST 1932 — FRIDAY
To Kapalga with five packs for salt. Note from J.A. gone to pull the dray out. Lost a black filly — suspect alligators.

14 AUGUST 1932 — SUNDAY
Took five packloads of salt over to new camp, where we saw tracks of big 'gator. Must poison him.

22 AUGUST 1932 — MONDAY
MV Maskee came in looking for Mole's camp. Arranged with J.A. to use his draught horses. My near side dray leader, Dolly, died here. Must have been bitten by snake.

23 AUGUST 1932 — TUESDAY
Maskee left on morning tide. Gaden came in from his camp. Sent one boy up the river for some more boys.

24 AUGUST 1932 — WEDNESDAY
No boys arrived today — this delay is driving me mad. This is now six days I've lost on this trip. Cannot get back to camp before the 26th now in any case.

25 AUGUST 1932 — THURSDAY
J.A. returned per canoe. *Maskee* has been on a mud bank for last three days. Sent up river by horse for blacks, may get them by tomorrow. Have lost a week now.

26 AUGUST 1932 — FRIDAY
Horses and several natives turned up at sundown. Gave P. Brady a job carting hides. Put four more blacks on. Packed up and started after sundown. Lost three horses, one with pack on, in scrub. Too dark so went back to Kapalga.

27 AUGUST 1932 — SATURDAY
Sent one boy after horses and packs that were lost last night. Left Brady to fetch dray and went on to camp. Arrived sundown. Horse called Pussy Cat died during absence.

28 August 1932 — Sunday
Two bulls, one cow. Dray not arrived yet. Should have been
here at midday.

29 August 1932 — Monday
Returned to camp at sundown and no sign of dray. So rode
back 12 miles along road and found dray on Flying Fox
Creek. One boy away after horses. Camped the night.

30 August 1932 — Tuesday
Brought dray into camp. Working five horses in harness now.

31 August 1932 — Wednesday
Four bulls, two cows. Left Brady and one boy at camp to put
up a rough yard for catching colts. Cracker nearly right now
and as fat as a seal.

6 September 1932 — Tuesday
Dray returned from Kapalga with five bags of salt. Word
from Howarth that he wants his horses back next week.
Damn him.

7 September 1932 — Wednesday
Brady breaking in grey mare.

8 September 1932 — Thursday
A touch of fever today, shooting very erratic. Horse called
Snowy down to it. Think she will die. Result of premature foal.

9 September 1932 — Friday
Still sick. Howarth turned up at camp this evening with
mail. Wants his horses back. Must go back and get more
from somewhere.

10 September 1932 — Saturday
Back to Kapalga with Howarth. Took one boy, four horses
and two packs.

12 September 1932 — Monday
Crossed Jim Jim and got to Yorky Bill's camp sundown.
Engaged Yorky Billy to run camp for me while away after
horses.

15 September 1932 — Thursday
From Barramundi Creek to South Alligator no water.
Arrived about 3.30 very thirsty. This river was running last
time I was here, almost dry now. Dolly's foal that followed
us is missing. Must have gone looking for water.

16 September 1932 — Friday
Arrived Goodparla. No horses available here. Got fresh
saddle horse. Left horses Flower and Rex until I return, also
one pack.

21 September 1932 — Wednesday
On to Jack Hore's place, found Dick Guild. Bought three
horses off J.A.

22 September 1932 — Thursday
Back to Guild's place, bought six more horses.

23 September 1932 — Friday
Left Guild, camped at Crocodile. Have eleven horses. On
half rations from now on — might make it last.

26 September 1932 — Monday
All day looking for horses Rex and Flower. Found them
myself at sundown. Boy still searching.

27 September 1932 — Tuesday
Camped Barramundi Creek. Sugar finished.

28 September 1932 — Wednesday
Camped Jim Jim. Tea finished.

29 SEPTEMBER 1932 — THURSDAY
Arrived Kapalga with just enough flour left for my meal.
Finished last of beef this morning.

30 SEPTEMBER 1932 — FRIDAY
Returned to camp; 46 hides shot during absence — very
satisfactory. Total 120 with 67 at landing. Box of dray wheel
giving trouble. Horse called Snowy died while away.

1 OCTOBER 1932 — SATURDAY
Started shooting again. Cloud is a very good shooting mare.

4 OCTOBER 1932 — TUESDAY
Horse called Cloud fell with me today. Must trim her hoofs
up. Short of salt.

5 OCTOBER 1932 — WEDNESDAY
Billy got a fall today. Dray not returned with salt so after
supper took pack horse and met dray at Flying Fox, about
midnight. Sent Spider to Gaden's camp for two bags of
flour.

6 OCTOBER 1932 — THURSDAY
Returned to camp with a pack load of salt. Spider returned
sundown reported Cracker bogged about eight miles away.
Too late to go tonight.

7 OCTOBER 1932 — FRIDAY
Went to Monassie Plain to get Cracker out. Worked all day
but horse too far gone. Too weak to sit up — put him out of
his misery. Another good horse gone.

9 OCTOBER 1932 — SUNDAY
While skinning a bull this morning, Spider drove his knife
into Billy's foot. Shooting suspended — 153 down with 105
at landing.

10 OCTOBER 1932 — MONDAY
No shooting. Building bark humpie in preparation for
approaching storms.

15 OCTOBER 1932 — SATURDAY
Returned to camp. Shot nine bulls and two cows — best day
yet. Had three falls today. Very sore.

24 OCTOBER 1932 — MONDAY
Loaded hides and went with dray to landing to meet boat.
Camped at Flying Fox.

25 OCTOBER 1932 — TUESDAY
Kapalga. Boys cutting paper bark and timber for hide house.
Killed a pig; 150 hides at landing.

27 OCTOBER 1932 — THURSDAY
Blackfellow turned up from Rindberg's camp with two
letters, both bills!

28 OCTOBER 1932 — FRIDAY
Sent boy to Rindberg's camp with letter. Trying to borrow
some rations. Dray turned up with 18 hides.

29 OCTOBER 1932 — SATURDAY
Boy returned from Rindberg's with 50 pound bag of flour
and some newspapers.

1 NOVEMBER 1932 — TUESDAY
Heavy storm over Flying Fox way last night. Unless boat
comes tomorrow will return to camp and ride into Darwin.

2 NOVEMBER 1932 — WEDNESDAY
Heavy rain last night. Self very bad with dysentery.

3 NOVEMBER 1932 — THURSDAY
Sent boy for dray. Down to it all day. Rations all finished.

4 NOVEMBER 1932 — FRIDAY
Much better this morning, still very weak. Paddy, the blackfellow, arrived with saddle and pack horses, so returned to camp.

5 NOVEMBER 1932 — SATURDAY
To Gaden's camp for Darwin mail. Gaden out, so left a note. No tucker left. Living on buffalo meat.

7 NOVEMBER 1932 — MONDAY
Packed up and left for Darwin, took two pack horses, four saddle horses and one boy. Camped half way between Alligator Creek and Cattle Creek. Storm.

8 NOVEMBER 1932 — TUESDAY
Horse called Spartan sick — left him on the Mary Plains. I suppose that's the last I'll see of him.

9 NOVEMBER 1932 — WEDNESDAY
Arrived Marrakai Station. Got some tea and sugar to see me into the telegraph line.

11 NOVEMBER 1932 — FRIDAY
Heavy storm last night. Got to Adelaide River siding after ploughing through 15 miles of water, which was up to horses' knees all the way.

12 NOVEMBER 1932 — SATURDAY
Left horses with Hazel Gaden and took train to Darwin.

13 NOVEMBER 1932 — SUNDAY
Drove out to Koolpinyah Station with Freddy Morris — partly broke axle in Howard Creek — walked 10 miles to station.

14 NOVEMBER 1932 — MONDAY
Darwin — waiting for boat to go out for hides.

C/- H J FOSTER
SOLICITOR
DARWIN

15 NOVEMBER 1932

Dear Mum

I have just returned to civilization after the shooting and have done fairly well, having shot 250 from September to October.

I am in Darwin at present but I'm going back to the Alligator River next Sunday to load my hides and fetch them in. Just at present I am very busy and hurrying to catch the aerial mail, which leaves shortly, as I know you will be anxious to hear from me.

With fondest love, your loving son

19 NOVEMBER 1932 — SATURDAY
Left Darwin per *MV Maroubra* for Alligator River.

21 NOVEMBER 1932 — MONDAY
Loaded 251 hides from my camp. Also 130 from Rindberg's landing. Paid off blacks and let them go bush for wet.

23 NOVEMBER 1932 — WEDNESDAY
Arrived Darwin and anchored.

6 DECEMBER 1932 — TUESDAY
Lads gave me a send-off tonight.
I decided to head west to the cattle country to see if I could pick up some work during the wet.

7 DECEMBER 1932 — WEDNESDAY
Took train to Adelaide River.

9 DECEMBER 1932 — FRIDAY
Mustered horses. One short — believed to be down Brocks Creek way — the bay mare, Kitten.

15 DECEMBER 1932 — THURSDAY
Ferguson River half way up saddle flaps. All rations wet.
Picked up Kitten from Fisher's Plant.

17 DECEMBER 1932 — SATURDAY
Got a change of horses and started for west.

18 DECEMBER 1932 — SUNDAY
Arrived Katherine River. Half a mile wide, so camped.

19 DECEMBER 1932 — MONDAY
Looking for horses. River dropped 3 feet during the night
but still too fast to swim horses.

20 DECEMBER 1932 — TUESDAY
River dropping fast. Collected four horses, one riding saddle.
I 'collected' the horses and saddle in payment for an unpaid debt.

21 DECEMBER 1932 — WEDNESDAY
Swam River after dinner and went about 6 miles and
camped.

25 DECEMBER 1932 — SUNDAY
Reached Willeroo Station. Xmas with old friends.

1933

1 JANUARY 1933 — SUNDAY
On to Victoria River Downs Station.

STURTS CREEK STATION
WESTERN AUSTRALIA

20 FEBRUARY 1933

Dear Mum

I promised to write to you and let you have some details of my shooting. I started to write you a letter in December and got about four pages of it done by February — when I finally went to finish it I found that the start was lost — so I am starting all over again.

I got 251 hides and they averaged a little over 72 pounds of weight per hide, which is a very good average, and at the price I got, they realised £327. After I got my share and squared up I had nothing left, but I didn't expect to have much as the expense of starting a plant is enormous. I had wages to pay and horses and gear to buy, and there was a lot of expense I never figured on but was necessary. However, I have a good plant now and the experience gained will be valuable for next time, if there is a next time. When I left Darwin hides had dropped to 2½ pence per pound, which as you can guess is no good.

I had a lot of disappointment and a lot of bad luck — some of my horses died and I had to buy more. However, I contracted to supply 200 hides and I got 250, and sold them all at a good price. I started shooting late in the season and had a lot of holdups. If I go out again and get a full season in, I could get 500 hides quite easily and what's more will be on my own.

I have not heard from Dora for a long time. I suppose she's got my photos by this time. I did them up and sent them in from Hunter's place to Darwin by a passing lugger, which put in for fresh water. I knew the chap and thought he was reliable, and gave him a few shillings to cover postage. However, he threw them into a corner of the place where he lodged in Darwin. He finally got kicked out for not paying his rent and after he had gone, the people sent the photos to me when I returned to town in November. I posted them myself straight away. I also put in a couple of local papers, which give an account of some recent native murders.

I got the offer of some horse breaking and am at Sturts Creek Station in Western Australia, and am starting to break in shortly. I have about 30 colts to do here, which at 25 shillings per head will be very handy and will keep the pot boiling until I start shooting again. I will probably break in horses at Flora Valley, but as soon as the price of hides rises I will go straight back to the coast. Since knocking off shooting I have ridden nearly 1000 miles, having come from 100 east of Darwin to Halls Creek (where this letter will be posted) and down to Sturts Creek Station.

Work is very scarce now and wages have come down to £2 per week, horse breaking being the only branch of station work that hasn't been chopped, and is always done contract (so much per head). I can break six colts a week fairly comfortably so you can see it is fair money. Sometimes we strike an outlaw and he lowers a man's average, but we have a way with them that steadies them down. But no matter how bad a horse is a breaker can refuse nothing and, of course, if he knows his job they don't worry him much.

By the way I sent you a Xmas present. I forget exactly what it's called, but it's supposed to be all right — it's made of crepe de something and is supposed to come from China. Hope it turns up all right.

There is not much more news to write about, so will close.

With much love to everybody, your loving son

DARWIN
NORTH AUSTRALIA

16 JUNE 1933

Dear Mum

Have just returned to Darwin from Western Australia, where I have been horse breaking since I knocked off shooting last year. Found your letters awaiting me in Darwin and also papers.

With regard to me trying to get on the films, I don't altogether care for the idea for several reasons. In the first place, I may not have the acting ability necessary to get on. In the second place, it would mean leaving my country for a year or so and I would probably lose it.

I now have a good strong plant of 30 to 40 horses, a dray, 11 sets of harness and five rifles. I have increased my holdings to 200 square miles and am slowly building up something. I like my horses and I like the life. I would like to come home and will, but don't want to throw up the substance for the shadow. Last year I went out and everyone prophesied that I would go broke and that there were no buffalo on the country I took up. I had a scratch plant and a late start, horses died and everything seemed against me, but in spite of it all I shot 250 hides. The result is that there were three applications laying in the lands office for Grazing Lease No. 693. I went to Western Australia and people thought I couldn't get back in time to pay my rent, however I did. This year I have the benefit of last year's experience, a stronger plant, an earlier start and I am on my own.

I have just returned from Darwin to Rutherven Station, a property belonging to a friend of mine, where I have had my horses running since last year. I have sent my supplies round to the Alligator River by lugger, half a ton of rations and four tons of salt. This is sufficient to salt 400 hides and I hope to have to order more salt before the year ends. Just at present, I am terribly busy getting my horses ready to start down. I have 150 miles to go and there are no roads in that country, so everything must be in apple pie order. So, we are busy mustering horses, shoeing horses, repairing gear, making hobbles, a colt or two to break in and so forth.

I really should write to Len and Phil, but I really haven't time as I am going all day and most of the night and hope to get away the day after tomorrow. I am writing this by the light of a slush lamp (a piece of rag stuck in a tin of fat).

One of the principal reasons why I am in such a hurry to get down there is I am afraid of other shooters encroaching on my country. There is very little legal redress because buffalo are game and the only thing you can go a man on is trespass.

I haven't heard from Uncle Tom for some time. I will write to him as soon as I am able. Will probably be able to write to you during the shoot as I have arranged for a lugger to come out twice for hides.

Goodbye and best love, your affectionate son

KAPALGA
NORTH AUSTRALIA

OCTOBER 1933

Dear Uncle Tom,

I will give you a brief summary of my last financial year, which may interest you. January 1st 1933 finds me full of new resolutions on my way to Western Australia looking for work to keep me going in the slack season. February finds me at Sturts Creek Station WA engaged in breaking in the rowdiest lot of colts that I've ever thrown a rope on to. I finished them by March. April, I did a few weeks mustering. May, I slung the packs on and returned to muster my own horses for the shooting. Between the time that I knocked off shooting last

FORM 16.

THE NORTHERN TERRITORY OF AUSTRALIA.

1931.
Crown Lands Ordinance ~~1924-1928~~.

Grazing Licence No. 716.

Licence to Graze Stock on Crown Lands for the period ending 30th June, 1934.

Whereas Thomas Ernest Cole ——————————————————

———————————————————————————————

———————————————————————————————

of Alligator River ——————————————————————

———————————————————————————————

———————————————————————————————

applied for a Licence to Graze Stock on Crown Lands. Now, therefore, in pursuance

1931
of the Crown Lands Ordinance ~~1924-1928~~ the said Thomas Ernest Cole —— —

———————————————————————————————

———————————————————————————————

hereby licensed to graze one hundred (100) .... head of stock

on the Crown Lands, comprising an area of one hundred (100) ————

square miles, as shown on the plan on the back hereof, from the

.... First .... day of .... July .... 1933 subject to

the provisions of the said Ordinance and the Regulations thereunder, at an annual

rental of Five Pounds (£5) plus One Pound (£1) licence fee.

DATED the Sixteenth day of June 1933.

(a) *[signature]*

Member of
Northern Territory Land Board.

(a) Seal of Land
Board or signa-
ture of person
authorised by
Board, as case
requires.

year and started this year, I had done over 1800 miles by horses, which is a big stage even for me.

I have taken up another 100 square miles, which makes my holding 200 square miles in all and, if things go favourably with me, I hope to take up a further 150 next year. I have been shooting since July 12th and will be finished by the end of this month, if I'm not carried away delirious before then. I have 312 shot to date and don't expect to have any trouble getting 400.

This year I have been able to employ a white man as cook, which has been a great help to me. He is an old musterer's cook whom I have known many years around the Victoria River district. It's a dog's life coming home at 9 and 10 o'clock — washing and salting hides, swallowing a drink of tea and a hunk of half cooked bread with salt buffalo, and then hopping in and cooking enough tucker for the camp for tomorrow. When I was shooting on the Adelaide River, the year before last, I was fortunate to get a lubra (native woman) clean and honest enough to leave in charge of the rations.

I am employing four boys, four lubras and one half-caste, who is a fairly good horseback shooter. Three of the boys and the half-caste (Yorky Billy) are 'married'. Two of the boys I've had in my camps for the last two years, and each season they've turned up 'married' to a different lubra.

16 OCTOBER

A friend of mine, a pearler in Darwin, had two of his pearling luggers — *Raf* and *Myrtle Olga* — put into Caledon Bay for water. The blacks cleaned up the two crews, except for one white, and a black fellow — seven in all. This occurred close to Millingimbe Mission. Then, this year a man named Jim Nicholls was speared in the Mainoru Station bullock paddock. This is a stone's throw from Roper River Mission. I knew Nicholls very well. When I was managing Bullita he built a stockyard for me — the yard we called Crisp's Yard — it was built on a spot where Jim Crisp was speared a few years previously when he (Crisp) was managing Bullita.

Now the latest sensation, and it takes a lot to cause a

sensation out here. A police party consisting of Mounted Constables Ted Morey (in charge), Vic Hall, Jack Mahoney, and McColl went out to get the murderers of the crews of the *Raf* and *Myrtle Olga*. They left the telegraph line the same time as I left to start shooting. We camped a night together on the Edith River and Morey bought two horses off me for the trip. Vic Hall and McColl went by lugger and Morey and Mahoney went overland. They met somewhere near Caedon Bay and while after some blacks, McColl got speared. The party, which was very badly equipped for an expedition of that nature, has returned. Of course there's a hell of a stink on now and I've heard from a reliable source that before he started on the expedition, Morey had applied for new fire arms and ammunition. This he was refused and McColl's revolver was found with three misfires, one chamber discharged and two undischarged. Of course, they're hushing it up.

Nine men have been speared now.

24 OCTOBER

I will try and send you some newspapers, so you can get an idea of public opinion.

The nearest policeman stationed around here is at Brocks Creek, and he does one patrol out this way every year. He is badly equipped, and he could not get back to his station this year without borrowing horses from Goodparla Station, to carry him the last 70 miles. He has, I suppose, one of the largest districts to patrol in the world. The Alligator River patrol alone covers about 600 miles, and this is usually curtailed on account of horses knocking up.

Well, suppose that after the constable had returned from his patrol that trouble had occurred somewhere and a white man had been speared. Fred Don, the policeman in question, didn't have one horse capable of carrying an empty saddle, much less following blacks over inaccessible country.

On the same boat that brought my mail, I had a friend come out for a visit. Fred Morris is an Administration Officer in Darwin and is at present on extended leave. He has been down

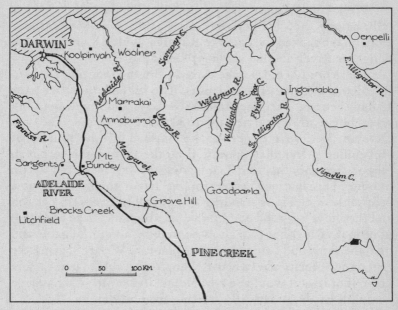

to Sydney for two months and is finishing his leave in my camp, having the time of his life. He brought out two cameras and has taken over 100 photos of buffalo shooting in all its phases, a lot of good nature studies, and photos of native corroboree etc. I will have some good pictures to send home later on, when they are developed and printed.

He also brought out an array of guns and the latest high-powered rifles. So far he hasn't succeeded in shooting a buffalo, but he's pretty well shot everything else, including one of my lads, who received a charge of number two shot and now has to have his meals standing up. He generally falls off his horse at least once a day and once a wounded buffalo chased him. He usually arrives home at the camp in a state of collapse and swears he is having the time of his life. Everybody's idea of a good time varies. Personally, my idea of good time would be some shady spot, a nice comfortable deck chair, and about five or six buxom wenches of about 18 summers keeping the iced drinks up. I could stand a lot of that.

Well, Uncle, since starting this letter, I have completed my tally having shot 402 buffalo between July 12th and October 25th. I have shifted the camp to Kapalga, which is on the South Alligator River and has the boat landing.

There are 120 hides to be carted from the shooting camp to Kapalga, a distance of 20 odd miles. This will take another 10 or 12 days because a trip occupies three days and my dray (a big seven horse affair) carries about 30 hides at a time. Today is October 31st, so I expect to be finished by the middle of November. After that there will be the wet season to put in (about five months) and I am going to try my hand at tin mining. This is a new game for me but it might turn out a profitable one. Tin is standing at something like £215 per ton and the show is a good one I think, all alluvial. There are three of us in it. The other two know something about the game and own the show and I am putting the plant in. We are sharing the remaining expenses between us. I hope to be able to make a few bob out of it — it would be a welcome lift for me — it has been an uphill battle, practically starting from nothing.

Thanks very much for the offer of the revolver, but I'm sorry I can't give you any information regarding duty and postal regulations and so forth. The nearest post office is something over 200 miles away. It would be very handy as I haven't got one. Where we are going for the wet, it's always advisable to keep a fire arm handy for a moral effect, and a rifle gets a bit tiring. You might be able to do something if you took the chamber out or the trigger or some other part of it and sent it half at a time. It wouldn't be a revolver then.

I am off to Darwin by the next lugger, which will probably take 100 of my hides, and back by the next boat, which will take the remainder of my hides (200) and make up a load from other shooters. So, I only expect to be in Darwin for a few days and will be pretty busy and don't expect to have time to write to everybody.

Your sincere nephew

P.S. Latest report on McColl trouble. The missionaries have offered to get the murderers of McColl and the crews of *Raf* and *Myrtle Olga*, and the Minister for the Interior has told them to get to it. The Rev. Dyer has charge of the party and says he feels God is with him, this is just as well, and he wants to keep Him near him.

C/- H. J. FOSTER
SOLICITOR
DARWIN
NORTH AUSTRALIA

20 NOVEMBER 1933

Dear Phyllis,

I have just received a letter from you dated 1/1/33, so you see it has taken a long time to reach me.

I have just finished the season's shoot, having got 402 hides, which is a very good season for me as far as the number of hides goes.

I am in a very isolated place, and I make arrangements for a lugger to cart my hides from the South Alligator River to Darwin. When I get out to my camp, I am entirely dependent on the lugger for supplies and for getting my hides into Darwin. I contracted to deliver 100 hides in Darwin by 6 August and 100 by the 6 September, but the lugger never came until 4 September. Fortunately, it didn't affect me regarding delivering hides, but we ran short of rations and worse than anything cartridges. However, everything came right in the end, so why worry.

I am glad to have knocked off so as to give my horses a much needed spell. They have been working very hard and I am now going to let them all rest and eat grass for the next six months, except for one. My favourite shooting horse, Black Eagle, I am lending to a friend in Darwin to race at the New Year meeting. This of course, won't do him any harm as he will be stabled and corn fed and looked after. After the races he will be sent out to Koolpinyah Station (a property owned by a friend of mine) to be turned out in the best paddock. I am now on my way out to a

tin show for the wet and I won't know how he got on until
May.

I daresay you have read about the various native murders
out my way; they seem to be arousing universal interest. A
couple of days ago, word came in that two more men have been
murdered. Two men, who were trepanging round the coast,
named Trynor and Fagan.

It appears they had been missing for some time, but their
half-burnt lugger and remains were found by a pearler and
trepanger named Gray. (Gray was the man who contracted
with me to cart my hides and salt.) Gray was anchored about
half a mile from the luggers *Raf* and *Myrtle Olga* last year when
the entire crews, except two, were wiped out by the same tribe.

A party of police, badly equipped for such an expedition,
left early this year to get the murderers of the two crews, but
they turned back from Woodah Island after one of the party,
Albert McColl, got speared through the heart.

The matter is causing a stir in this country now. The
Minister for the Interior has accepted the offer of a party of
missionaries to go down and herd the blacks into Darwin
without bloodshed. The general opinion is that there will be a
few missionaries less in the world before it is all over.

Well, I'm afraid that these few items of blood curdling
news are about all I can find to write about, so will close with
best love.

Your affectionate brother

DARWIN
NORTH AUSTRALIA

DECEMBER 1933

Dear Mum,

I now have an interest in a tin mine which should prove a good
proposition. Tin is at £224 per ton which is the best price it's
been since the war. It is an alluvial show. We are going to put
sluice boxes in and work it during the wet season.

We hope to get three tons. There are three of us in it. I am putting in the equipment and we are bearing the running expenses between us.

I have 100 miles to take my dray loaded with six months supplies. The wet season is right on our heels and we are already getting heavy storms everyday. I expect to have to cut a road for about 30 miles through some bad scrub. I have a big river (the East Alligator) to cross and I am anxious to push on and cross it before it rises. I will be absolutely marooned for the wet and will have no means of communication until about April or May. All the rivers and creeks will be impassable until then. However I will be quite satisfied to put up with all that if we get the tin.

My love to everybody and a Merry Christmas to all. I will be out in the Arnhem Land waiting for Father Christmas to fill my stockings up with tin.
Fondest love

1934

1 JANUARY 1934 — MONDAY
No good resolutions to record, in fact, distinctly the reverse.
Buckboard wheel (which was broken on 27 December while
buckboard was bogged to the axle) is progressing favourably
with seven spokes finished. Dave and Charlie finished the
ninth spoke, wheel to be assembled tomorrow.

2 JANUARY 1934 — TUESDAY
Wheel finished. Went out to pick a track along the ridges to
avoid bog. Blazed a good line.

3 JANUARY 1934 — WEDNESDAY
Decided to lighten load from buckboard, so Charlie and I packed
up seven horses and went on ahead leaving Dave at camp. Took
Whalebone the black boy. Travelled about 17 miles.

4 JANUARY 1934 — THURSDAY
Travelled about 14 miles and decided to camp on a creek,
which may be Magela Creek. Will leave our load here (10
bags of flour and some salt) and return for buckboard.

5 JANUARY 1934 — FRIDAY
Stacked flour and covered it up with bark and made back.
Grey horse dropped dead at dinner camp. Dragon also
knocked up. Horses getting weak. Too much bog. Rained
during early part of night.

8 JANUARY 1934 — MONDAY

Beef finished. Decided to try Emblem as shooting horse with disastrous results. Horse wouldn't go up to bull, so chased it for about 3 miles through thick scrub and lost it in cane grass swamp. Later, I saw some cows on the opposite side of big swamp and by the time I got round they were gone. Too dark by this time to track. Lost pack horse in thick scrub on the way home.

9 JANUARY 1934 — TUESDAY

Horse lost last night turned up this morning with pack on and breeching straps broken. Made a start with buckboard. Travelled about 6 miles. Some heavy scrub cutting through here. Dave found two pieces of smoked salt beef in a pack bag. Loud cheers.

11 JANUARY 1934 — THURSDAY

Very good day. Charlie Burns driving buckboard self cutting track went about 8 miles. Damper and jam diet. Game very scarce on the ridges at this time of the year.

12 JANUARY 1934 — FRIDAY

Heavy rain last night made travel impossible, again. Boy returned with pack horses and reports Peggy, a good draft mare, knocked up.

13 JANUARY 1934 — SATURDAY

More rain last night. While cutting and blazing track I saw buffalo track, so went back to camp for rifle. Struck a mob of fat cows in heavy bog and consequently lost them.

14 JANUARY 1934 — SUNDAY

Abandoned buckboard. Packed everything possible. Found Peggy down to it and had to shoot the poor brute — one of my best horses. Shot buffalo cow.

15 JANUARY 1934 — MONDAY
Horse called Dragon found dead this morning. This is the
result of travelling horses through bog in the wet season.
This morning found that the creek we are camped on is a
tributary of Magela Creek, which is about 2 miles over.
Walked over and found Magela running a banker [bank to
bank].

16 JANUARY 1934 — TUESDAY
Blazed track across to Magela and decided to shift over onto
it and wait for it to fall. This creek comes out of the ranges
and rises and falls very quickly, current very fast. We can
hear it roaring all night. Probably heavy rain at the head.

18 JANUARY 1934 — THURSDAY
Crossed Magela Creek with water half way up to saddle
flaps but managed to keep everything dry. Blow flies here in
their millions, so have to keep beef in heavy smoke. Sleeping
blankets and saddle blankets are all flyblown. Dave had to
throw one of his blankets away, which was promptly
grabbed by a blackfella.

19 JANUARY 1934 — FRIDAY
Charlie Burns and I took six pack loads across to make a
camp on East Alligator River. Camped within 3 miles of
river, so I took a boy and walked down but could only get to
outside channel, which was running a banker. Mobs of bush
blacks camped about here. One lot have a tree down and are
making a canoe. Heavy storm.

20 JANUARY 1934 — SATURDAY
Left Charlie and returned for rest of camp. Struck Surveyor
Blain marooned by wet at Jabiluka (with his field assistant)
so camped the night with him swapping lies. I have one of
my buffalo camp boys with me — Tommy.

22 JANUARY 1934 — MONDAY
Took Tommy and one pack back to buckboard for a few
articles. Got to buckboard about sundown and found it a
morass of water bog.

23 JANUARY 1934 — TUESDAY
Camped Magela crossing on return journey. Broke a mirror
— this is the second this year — I wonder if the sentences
are concurrent or cumulative!

25 JANUARY 1934 — THURSDAY
Charlie and I assisted blacks (principally by directions) to
finish their canoe and hauled it down to river with a harness
mule. Intend using it to cross the river tomorrow. Found
good place to swim horses — I hope the alligators are in a
sociable frame of mind.

26 JANUARY 1934 — FRIDAY
Crossed saddles, gear and equipment in dugout canoe and swam
horses successfully. Boy shot bull buffalo. Tough but acceptable.

27 JANUARY 1934 — SATURDAY
Tommy and Whalebone and his lubra left last night. They
took canoe and left it on the opposite side. Swam river and
followed them nine miles, but lost tracks in the ranges. I
went into surveyor's camp and had a late breakfast (1.30
p.m.). Borrowed horse rode back. River rising.

28 JANUARY 1934 — SUNDAY
Bad day. Charlie and I started up river (it runs through a
gorge here) with packs. Half mile up had to unpack and
carry everything across deep channel. After a further mile
had to make paperbark raft and swim horses. After dinner
left Charlie and went back for canoe but current too strong,
so camped with Dave for the night. Put eight more boys on,
making ten in all. Will pack everything up and go to Charlie
tomorrow with boys. River still rising.

29 JANUARY 1934 — MONDAY
Shifted rest of camp up, each boy carrying 50 lb. The first
bad channel, which had about 5 feet 5 inches of water
yesterday, has about 7 feet in the middle today. Boys walked
under the water and carried everything over their heads,
clear of the water. Camped in a very low place. God help us
if the river rises 4 feet tonight. She's roaring through these
ranges like a locomotive gone mad.

30 JANUARY 1934 — TUESDAY
Packed seven horses and six boys this morning, and went
about 3 miles, after much trouble packing and unpacking.
Swam horses round a rocky point where gorge comes right
in to main channel and carried everything through narrow
crevice about a foot wide. Got through the gorge and
camped at the junction of Alligator River and creek which
heads into the tin country. This creek that we have to follow
is a mile wide here. Light steady rain.

31 JANUARY 1934 — WEDNESDAY
River still rising. Raining on and off all of last night. All our
tents are leaking. Everything damp and mildewed. Flour going
green. Boys made a paperbark raft to cross everything over.
Tried to swim horses but forced back. Water is running up the
creek owing to river being in flood. Tried to find a track up
this side of creek but inaccessible as ranges come right into the
main channel. I will try and make a big raft and float up
stream. Beef finished. Boy went out with shotgun and spear
and returned with three geese and quantity of fish. Raining.

1 FEBRUARY 1934 — THURSDAY
River held her own last night. I made a large paperbark raft.
Very rainy weather.

2 FEBRUARY 1934 — FRIDAY
Charlie took two boys and put a small load on raft and
started off to cross plain. Later I climbed up on a hill and

saw his fly rigged about a mile and half over. Later found a
big tree about 3 foot through so cut it down to make a
canoe. The two boys who went with Charlie returned about
sundown. Will probably have to walk the rest of the way
and carry everything. River rose another two feet today.
First fine day, although appeared to be a storm up the river.

3 FEBRUARY 1934 — SATURDAY
River still rising steadily. Water dangerously close to camp.
Tree we cut down last night, which was growing at water's
edge, now submerged. Took six boys and went across to
Charlie's camp and started to walk to tin deposit. We went
about a mile and had to make paperbark raft to cross creek.
Crossed and camped.

4 FEBRUARY 1934 — SUNDAY
Three boys ran away last night. Sent rest of boys out
hunting, owing to beef shortage. They returned with a
wallaby.

5 FEBRUARY 1934 — MONDAY
I gave Charlie Burns a start and decided to go back to camp
and try and get horses across. On my return, Dave told me
the boys that ran away turned up late that night and said
that I'd sent them back for shotgun, cartridges, matches and
tomahawk! River started to fall.

6 FEBRUARY 1934 — TUESDAY
Started to chop canoe out this morning. A heavy storm in
the afternoon held up operations. River still falling. Outside
flats are uncovered.

7 FEBRUARY 1934 — WEDNESDAY
Got a full day in cutting out canoe. Damn tough timber.
About an inch of rain fell at sundown.

8 FEBRUARY 1934 — THURSDAY
Chopping out canoe. Tree seems to be getting tougher —
probably because our tools are getting blunt and we've
nothing to sharpen them with. Starting to weaken on this
bread and fat diet. I suppose we are lucky to have fat.

9 FEBRUARY 1934 — FRIDAY
Worked on the canoe in the morning. After dinner scouted
up some blacks and sent them out hunting but they came
back with nothing. Grass is about 8 feet high. The river's
getting low enough and should be able to swim horses
tomorrow.

10 FEBRUARY 1934 — SATURDAY
Worked on canoe in the morning. Tried to cross horses after
dinner but only got them across the outside flat. Bogged to
their flanks all the way. The plain is almost clear of water,
although ground boggy. Most of waters are confined to main
channels.

11 FEBRUARY 1934 — SUNDAY
Swam horses across main channel and crossed second
channel. Finished canoe.

12 FEBRUARY 1934 — MONDAY
Launched canoe and took it across creek and onto the
swamps to see if we could cross plain but the water is
coming down too strong. Plan of present situation. Charlie
Burns has walked up to tin show [deposit] and left Dave and
I at X to cross horses and plant.

19 FEBRUARY 1934 — MONDAY
Met Charlie who had left the tin camp and come back 8
miles looking for beef. He says tin very poor and won't clear
expenses. He intends prospecting surrounding country,
which indicates tin deposits.

2nd Month	FEBRUARY 1934	28 Days

12 MONDAY 43-322

Launched canoe & took it across creek &
onto the swamps to see if we could cross
plain but water coming down too strong

Plan of present
situation Charlie
Burns has walked
up to tin show &
left canoe & I at x to
cross lines & plant

13 TUESDAY 44-321

Started to shift camp up the river with canoe
but heavy rain came up before I got more than a mile so
stacked everything on the bank, covered it up with
a tarpaulin & returned to camp.

14 WEDNESDAY 45-320
Ash Wednesday, 1st Day in Lent

Picked up yesterdays load dumped it at a suitable
camp two miles up the river. Tried to take
another load after dinner but it rained too
heavy. Boys who walked up with Charlie returned
with letter saying country very boggy & one
very fast dangerous creek to cross

20 FEBRUARY 1934 — TUESDAY

Charlie is prospecting and got some colours in one dish of dirt.

21 FEBRUARY 1934 — WEDNESDAY

Charlie again out prospecting this morning but traced nothing. Heavy rain after dinner.

22 FEBRUARY 1934 — THURSDAY

All creeks running a banker; more rain. Beef all turning rotten. Our old friends the blowflies are well represented.

23 FEBRUARY 1934 — FRIDAY

Went down the creek to try and get another buffalo. Bog everywhere. Returned with nothing.

24 FEBRUARY 1934 — SATURDAY

Decided to shift up to tin camp and try and make the best of it. I may get enough tin out to pay the rent, which is as much as I hope for.

26 FEBRUARY 1934 — MONDAY

Took packs across to Coopers Creek, camped Nimbawah. Passed three black camps, about 100 blacks all told, very few of whom can speak English. A good few followed me down to be in at the kill.

27 FEBRUARY 1934 — TUESDAY

Although I can travel by following the bank of the creek, which is hard red clay, the country off the creek is too boggy for horses to travel, so could not go out after buffalo with horses. Pitched a camp early this morning about 5 miles from Nimbawah. Gave my boy, Cockeye, the rifle and sent him out on foot. Could not go myself as bush blacks would have cleaned my camp up. About ten of Cockeye's brethren also went.

28 FEBRUARY 1934 — WEDNESDAY
Cockeye got back at sundown tonight with three bags of
beef. Salted all of it. Good 28th birthday present. Old age is
creeping on.

1 MARCH 1934 — THURSDAY
Back to the camp. Good storm this morning. Creek running
too strong to cross, so can't go back for Dave and the rest of
the camp. Charlie has picked out a gully to work on, which
is showing a light prospect of 1 to 2 ounces to the dish.

2 MARCH 1934 — FRIDAY
Started working. Put a dam across and started stripping
creek bed. There's tin here all right, but all Arnhem Land is
mixed with it and the separating process won't be a
profitable one.

5 MARCH 1934 — MONDAY
Cleaning out creek bed. Boy turned up with SOS from
Dave, who has neither beef nor cartridges. Sent him back
some cartridges.

6 MARCH 1934 — TUESDAY
Sent a boy to Oenpelli Mission to try and get some papers
and find out if any luggers are expected from Darwin.
Cockeye ran away this morning.

7 MARCH 1934 — WEDNESDAY
Made another start to Dave's camp. Creek still fairly high.
Made paperbark raft and crossed with swag and rations.
Horses were just able to walk across. Creek running very
fast. Camped at the foot of the range. Heavy rain.

8 MARCH 1934 — THURSDAY
Arrived at Dave's camp. Tucker getting low. Dave has one
bag of flour left (50 pounds) and no sugar. Half a bag of
sugar (35 pounds) and one bag of flour are up at tin camp.

Owing to the flour having got wet so often we are losing 20 pounds of flour out of each 50. There is fully this amount of hard yellow lumps. We are saving the lumps to grind-up later on. The sugar has sweated away.

9 MARCH 1934 — FRIDAY
I gave boys (who are camped here) some salt and a rifle and sent them across to the other side of the swamps to try and get a buffalo.

10 MARCH 1934 — SATURDAY
Bread and fat diet; tea without sugar.

11 MARCH 1934 — SUNDAY
Shot a pigeon with last shotgun cartridge.

12 MARCH 1934 — MONDAY
Boys returned without beef.

13 MARCH 1934 — TUESDAY
Sunk the canoe before daylight this morning in shallow water where I can easily get it up again. May require it later to get tin down to the lugger landing, but won't have it if I leave it here with these blacks. Been puzzling my head about this last week as to where to hide it. I think I have solved the problem.

14 MARCH 1934 — WEDNESDAY
Packed up everything and made a start for the tin camp. Camped at the foot of the range; it rained all the afternoon. Both Dave and I are weak for the want of a square meal.

15 MARCH 1934 — THURSDAY
Arrived at the tin camp. While Charlie was down working in the creek yesterday, blacks raided the camp and got away with some rations and about half of his swag! Received some three month old papers from Oenpelli.

16 MARCH 1934 — FRIDAY
Installed a banjo this morning and banjoed first lot of dirt.
Results are not very promising. Took packs and went out to
try and get some beef.

17 MARCH 1934 — SATURDAY
Walked all day with two boys tracking a mob of buffalo
cows. Came up to them twice but could not get a shot. Grass
fully ten feet high. I am down to two feeds a day until I
return to camp.

18 MARCH 1934 — SUNDAY
Got a shot at a bull this morning — followed a trail of blood
all day — camped on his tracks without swag or tucker.
Rained all night.

19 MARCH 1934 — MONDAY
Followed wounded bull until we were too knocked up to go
further. We've had nothing to eat since yesterday morning.
On our way back to the camp we got a kangaroo with a
broken leg — providence! — had a feed and packed up the
horses and went back to the tin camp. Dave made a stew of
the tail, and we salted some and gave the rest to the blacks.
Raining.

20 MARCH 1934 — TUESDAY
It rained all of last night and all day. Feet swollen from my
weekend jaunt.

22 MARCH 1934 — THURSDAY
We started grinding up the yellow lumps of flour in the
mincing machine, fortunately, we had saved most of these
lumps.

24 MARCH 1934 — SATURDAY
Charlie took three packs and tried to get through to
Oenpelli for rations and beef. Weather cleared.

25 MARCH 1934 — SUNDAY
Sent boy out with rifle and he returned with two wallabies.
Later, bush black turned up with some buffalo beef, which
he said blacks had speared at Coopers Creek. A feast or a
famine!

26 MARCH 1934 — MONDAY
Working in the tin gully — put two holes down into creek
bed about two feet — dirt carrying good tin. Will sink
down tomorrow and try and get to creek bed. I've had the
unusual experience of three good consecutive feeds.
Weather cleared — wet season appears to have broken.

29 MARCH 1934 — THURSDAY
Counterlining pack-saddle. Back on bread diet. The colour
of the bread is a dirty yellow! Dingoes howling all night.
Out with the rifle but only saw two rock wallabies and I
couldn't get a shot at them. Blacks fetching in a few yams
and small fish in exchange for tobacco.

30 MARCH 1934 — FRIDAY
Boy arrived from Oenpelli with bag of beef and note from
Charlie, saying he got to Oenpelli after three hard days
battling through bog; horses are knocked up, so giving them
a few days spell before he starts back. Finished pack-saddle
— only two more to do. Dave put out some strychnine baits
for dingoes.

1 APRIL 1934 — SUNDAY
Boy found a dog, which was poisoned night before last.
Shifted all the Coopers Creek blacks — getting too cheeky
for my peace of mind.

2 APRIL 1934 — MONDAY
Working in tin gully. Creek bed going down. This wash is
carrying the best tin we've seen so far, it is very rich dirt.
As we are on the verge of starvation, we will be unable to

work it right out and nothing will drag me back into this country!

4 APRIL 1934 — WEDNESDAY
Screening wash. Beef finished. Blackfellow brought a wallaby in and we took the tail. I wonder where the next feed is coming from? I've never seen a country so devoid of game as this one is here. Charlie Burns is well overdue; whatever is keeping him?

5 APRIL 1934 — THURSDAY
Charlie arrived back about 2 o'clock today with a pack load of beef and a bag of flour, some rice and, best of all, some vegetables, with a bit of religion chucked in for good measure.

9 APRIL 1934 — MONDAY
Oiling and greasing gear and packing up preparatory to start tomorrow. Charlie dressed the tin we got (about 30 lb). Light storm after dinner. Dave put some more baits out to give the dogs a final go.

10 APRIL 1934 — TUESDAY
Packed up and got away with a good early start. Two of Dave's baits gone but we didn't have time to look for any dogs. Travelled about 12 miles and camped. Light storm.

11 APRIL 1934 — WEDNESDAY
Rained on and off last night — not enough to do any harm. Went on to the river and camped. After dinner, Charlie and I went over to where I'd sunk the canoe and bailed it out.

12 APRIL 1934 — THURSDAY
Digging canals and making dams to raise water level and got the canoe within ten yards of the river. Picked up a boy and gave him a job as far as Magela Creek as a pilot. We are going back a different way and none of us know the country.

13 APRIL 1934 — FRIDAY
Got the canoe into the river and crossed with packs, saddles
and other gear — swam horses safely over.

20 APRIL 1934 — FRIDAY
Charlie Burns and I took a pack and went across to where
we left the buckboard. Flats and creeks are still too boggy to
take buckboard back, so we decided to leave it until the
country dries up a bit.

23 APRIL 1934 — MONDAY
Struck a good deal of bog and water today. Camped Jim Jim
Creek. Finished sugar. Only one baking of flour left.

24 APRIL 1934 — TUESDAY
I took one pack across to Umalbar mine to try and get some
rations to carry us across to Kapalga, but found them right
out of everything except beef. Company aeroplane missing
and truck out of order. The manager sent packhorses 100
miles into Pine Creek to relieve situation. Women are here
with babies, so left them what tea and bread I had. First
white women I have seen since November.

25 APRIL 1934 — WEDNESDAY
I returned to camp. On my way back struck blacks and
traded a stick of twist for a good ten pound fish. Only dry
salt-beef and tea left in the camp, now.

26 APRIL 1934 — THURSDAY
Went out this morning to try and get some beef with no luck.
Packed up after dinner and pushed on — crossed South Alligator
River — camped on a swamp lower down. Plenty of bog and
water. This country will take another six weeks to dry.

27 APRIL 1934 — FRIDAY
We left the South Alligator fall as too much bog and water.
Crossed the dividing range that separates the South Alligator

and West Alligator Rivers and camped on the head of West
Alligator River.

28 APRIL 1934 — SATURDAY
Followed West Alligator River down and picked up an old
buffalo camp road, where I had been carting hides, and got
to Kapalga. The man in charge is just off with packs to try
and get rations. We got half a pumpkin and some buffalo
beef.

29 APRIL 1934 — SUNDAY
Turned all the horses out for badly needed spell. Mustered
the horses left here in December — one horse short —
alligators may have got him.

30 APRIL 1934 — MONDAY
Some buffalo camp boys including my right hand boy
(Singing Man Billy) came up the river in a canoe from Field
Island. Gave Billy a rifle and sent him down the river for a
buffalo. I expect him to be back in four days. I cleaned and
oiled four .303s, one shotgun and two .22 rifles. A bad boil is
coming up on my foot.

1 MAY 1934 — TUESDAY
Cleaned and oiled four .303s, two .22s and one shotgun. Boil
is still boiling.

3 MAY 1934 — THURSDAY
We got some fresh horses in-hand. Our situation is getting
serious — we are living on wallabies and jungle fowl — the
lugger from Darwin should have been here about the 24th of
last month. Dave and Charlie are out of tobacco.

4 MAY 1934 — FRIDAY
Killed a pig.

6 MAY 1934 — SUNDAY
Getting horses for road-plant for trip to Pine Creek.

7 MAY 1934 — MONDAY
Killed a big brown snake right in the camp today. Turned
out to be a Taipan. Snakes very plentiful here this year.

8 MAY 1934 — TUESDAY
Packed up and made a start for Pine Creek.

9 MAY 1934 — WEDNESDAY
Put myself on two feeds a day to try and make what little bit
of pork I have last. We had to make a thirty mile detour to
get round the swamps — more water than I have ever seen
before. Twelve solid hours in the saddle without a break —
horses are very tired. Camped on the head of the Red Lily
Swamps.

10 MAY 1934 — THURSDAY
Got round the swamps this morning and into high country
and back to the river. Shot a scrub bull after dinner and
turned out early and repaired the wasted tissues with grilled
steak.

11 MAY 1934 — FRIDAY
Pushed on up the river this morning and passed Konkamorla
and camped at the Wire Yard. Matches cut out today —
carrying a firestick.

12 MAY 1934 — SATURDAY
I arrived at Goodparla Station. I hoped to get enough flour
and sugar etc. to see me to Pine Creek, but nobody home.
Got a couple of pumpkins from the garden.

13 MAY 1934 — SUNDAY
Went to Little Mary River. Met Yorky Mick, who was out
of rations, and got half a box of matches off him.

15 MAY 1934 — TUESDAY

Arrived at Pine Creek. Got 30 shillings for the tin! Everyone is gold mad here. Unless you can talk about gossan quartz, micaceous schist or refractory ore you're right out of it here. I think the pub is the best claim in Pine Creek. Everyone is perpetually thirsty.

DARWIN
NORTH AUSTRALIA
20 MAY 1934

Dear Mum,

Arrived back in Darwin and have just opened your lovely present.

Sorry to have to tell you this but we did absolutely no good in the wet and got no tin. I am pretty well broke now and have to make a fresh start. Of course, I still have my plant. I returned to Pine Creek with packhorses and caught the train from there, and got to Darwin last night (Saturday). The shooting season starts about this time of the year and I have come down to see the buyers. The general prevailing impression is by no means optimistic and I'm afraid I may have to have a look around and find something else.

There are a few of us here who are trying to develop a market for alligator hides. A trial shipment sent away at the end of last year went very well.

Today is Sunday, and on Monday morning I will have the wires running hot wiring for quotations and if I can secure a definite price will give them a go.

We had a pretty rough time in the wet, which never eased up until the end of March. We ran out of rations and were just living on the rifle.

I am going to write to Peggy as soon as I can, but I'm sure you have no idea what a business it is going out bush for six months — ordering stores, and arranging for a lugger; liaising with agents, aboriginal departments, the lands office, bank and

stores; and doing a hundred and one other things in Darwin.
After I've done all this, I'm off to Pine Creek on Wednesday
morning (146 miles) and have horses to muster and shoe, and
blacks to find.

I have just seen a few of the photos that my friend, Freddy
Morris, took when out in my camp. He sent some to the English
Daily Express and the Times, which you may see published.
They were all taken at my camp and on my country around the
Wildman River.

Written later

As you may possibly remember me telling you, I have a white
man in my camp, an old chap I have known for years and he
doesn't want to leave me. His name is Dave Cameron and he is
a genuine old bushman, who has been cooking for drovers,
mustering camps and shearers all over Australia. As a matter of
fact, I am not really in a position to employ a cook, but it is very
nice to come home completely knocked up at night and know
there is a good feed waiting.

Later

Owing to unforeseen circumstances I have had to stop in town
another week, but I'm hoping to get away on a special train
that leaves Darwin on Tuesday.

21 MAY 1934 — MONDAY

Saw Fawcett regarding my account, a credit balance! —
wonders never cease! Saw Lands Office. Received offer from
Freer to shoot 500 hides contract. Wired Johnson in Sydney
and Nathan in Melbourne regarding alligator hides and
received favourable replies.

22 MAY 1934 — TUESDAY

Accepted Freer's offer. Saw Fawcett regarding rations and
loading. Saw Bert Wills and arranged for him to cart
loading in his lugger, the *Chantress*. Saw bank! Ordered five
tons of salt from salt worker.

23 MAY 1934 — WEDNESDAY
Owing to pressure of business unable to catch train — no
more trains until next Wednesday. I received a favourable
quotation from alligator buyers.

29 MAY 1934 — TUESDAY
Saw Constable Fitzgerald regarding Bill Jenning's mare that
was wrongly branded by Jim Moles who was killed by a
buffalo last year. Wrote Bill.

30 MAY 1934 — WEDNESDAY
I returned to Pine Creek. I got a boy to work as horse tailer.
His name is Peter; wife is called Rosie and offspring, Bobby.

2 JUNE 1934 — SATURDAY
Word came through from Darwin this afternoon that a
native boy called Butcher ran amok in Gaden's buffalo
camp. He shot and killed Bill Jennings and one lubra. He
blew half of Jack Gaden's hand off and wounded another
lubra and has gone bush with a .303 rifle and belt of
cartridges.

3 JUNE 1934 — SUNDAY
I took a colt out on the track for a trial. It ran off the track
and I fell at full gallop, which put me in bed.

4 JUNE 1934 — MONDAY
I'm still in bed from fall. I wired administrator to send
someone round to Kapalga by launch. Dave Cameron is
there on his own. Butcher will make straight for Kapalga as
this is his country.

5 JUNE 1934 — TUESDAY
Received reply from inspector of police, which was very
unsatisfactory, so I wired again. The lubra that was
wounded by Butcher has died — three deaths, now.

6 JUNE 1934 — WEDNESDAY
No reply from Darwin. Rang up and got Sergeant
Bridgeland on the phone and tells me Langdon leaving for
Kapalga by lugger tomorrow. Wanted to know could I let
them have horses. Told him to take whatever he wanted.
Still in bed.

7 JUNE 1934 — THURSDAY
Started to hobble about on a stick, very stiff and sore.

9 JUNE 1934 — SATURDAY
I'm walking quite well today. I rode a horse up to town and
as I came close to the pub someone shouted, 'Last past the
pub shouts!' — I was first! Snowy Bryant is coming as far as
Umalbar with me; we're starting tomorrow.

14 JUNE 1934 — THURSDAY
Sent a bush blackfella across to Monty Sullivan, the
manager, on the Mary River regarding some colts he has
promised me for six months if I break them in. Went out for
a killer for camp beef. Gave Cooke a hand to brand a few
calves.

17 JUNE 1934 — SUNDAY
Started breaking in the horses.

20 JUNE 1934 — WEDNESDAY
Packed up and left Goodparla with 15 head of horses and
two packs. Camped at Nine Mile.

26 JUNE 1934 — TUESDAY
Camped on the edge of the plains on the Ingarrabba Point.
Chestnut filly knocked-up today while carrying a pack and
had to leave her. We found an emu's nest with nine eggs and
had visions of sponge cakes and omelettes, but they were just
on the point of hatching.

27 JUNE 1934 — WEDNESDAY
Reached Kapalga for dinner and found Dave out of tucker
and the boat hadn't arrived. The boat left Darwin on June
7th. Went out after dinner and had a look at horses that
were left here. Found Dynamite dead, Ladybird with two
swamp cancers, and Demon sick with strangles and Spark
looking like a hunted devil. Yarded Ladybird. Operate
tomorrow.

28 JUNE 1934 — THURSDAY
Operated on Ladybird this morning. Went out later and got
Storm, Wallaby and Chester. Storm and Wallaby are fat;
Chester is in a fair condition. Found Bally and Crow in very
poor condition, with no hope of working them for several
months. All the horses appear to have had strangles and most
of them are very weak, and I can't find several of them.

29 JUNE 1934 — FRIDAY
Tim Blackman walked in about dinner time with good news
— the boat has arrived. It is anchored down stream waiting
for the tide to turn. Tim has come over to muster horses for
Gaden. The boat came up to the landing at about 10 o'clock.

30 JUNE 1934 — SATURDAY
Unloaded boat this morning, then went out after the missing
horses after dinner with no luck.

6 JULY 1934 — FRIDAY
Found three horses after dinner — one old mare and a horse
belonging to Gaden and one colt of Charlie Burns'. Returned
to camp very disappointed. Crow, my harness horse, died
the day I got back. Probably from strangles. I hadn't seen
him for a week and he was very low then.

9 JULY 1934 — MONDAY
Had to shoot Ladybird this morning. Cancer too far gone.

10 JULY 1934 — TUESDAY
Found the Bally horse dead. This leaves me two horses
broken in to harness, out of seven.

11 JULY 1934 — WEDNESDAY
Rode about 35 miles today trying to find horses. Horse
situation is very serious as I will need every horse I have
before I get 500 hides.

13 JULY 1934 — FRIDAY
Rode all the morning but found nothing — no fresh tracks,
so returned to camp. Some blacks turned up this evening:
Government and his lubra Nancy, Wallaby, Sligo and One
Eye. I put on Wallaby, Sligo and Government and his
spouse.

17 JULY 1934 — TUESDAY
Left this morning with Tim Blackman for Marrakai Station.
Will try and get some donkeys off Hazel Gaden to see me
through the season, and might pick up some more blacks
over on the Mary River.

18 JULY 1934 — WEDNESDAY
Camped on the edge of the Mary River Plains. Picked up
Isobell here, a mare of mine I lost two years ago.

20 JULY 1934 — FRIDAY
I got the loan of a roan harness horse from Hazel Gaden,
together with Eagle, my shooting horse, which Hazel took
to race after we knocked off shooting last year.

24 JULY 1934 — TUESDAY
Shifted over to Jimmy Stott's shooting camp at Red Lily. No
blacks here, so I will not be able to take donkeys. It is
impossible to drive a mob of horses and donkeys single-
handed. It is a three man job at any time.

25 July 1934 — Wednesday
Packed up this morning and started back to the camp. A
wasted trip. Camped Wild Boar Lagoon.

27 July 1934 — Friday
Arrived camp about sundown and found my foot-shooter
(Singing Man Billy) had turned up with a couple of mates
(Paddy and Bobby). Billy has taken unto himself another
wife since last year. Peter found colt called Snake while I
was away apparently been torn by an alligator about six
weeks ago. Wound almost healed.

1 August 1934 — Wednesday
A lot of horses cleared out last night owing to the scarcity of
horse feed. Went out for a ride to try and locate some better
country — not much grass about as buffalo have got the
country cleaned up. Got back to the camp and found that
Dick Guild had turned up with 15 head of fat horses for me.
I never needed them more in my life.

11 August 1934 — Saturday
Started shooting and put up a record — 25 in two runs. The
shooting horse is going well. Couldn't get all the hides into
camp today. Got them all skinned by working all day till
dark, without dinner. Left seven hides to be brought in
tomorrow.

14 August 1934 — Tuesday
Dick went with one boy back to Kapalga for fresh horses.
Twelve heavy hides. The brown shooting horse is getting
frightened of buffalo as too many bulls are charging.

15 August 1934 — Wednesday
Left the shooting horse home today and went foot shooting
through the scrub.

18 AUGUST 1934 — SATURDAY
Went foot shooting today and was jammed up between a
couple of bulls — things were very touchy for a few
seconds.

31 AUGUST 1934 — FRIDAY
Boat due any day now so returned to main camp to cart
hides.

1 SEPTEMBER 1934 — SATURDAY
Carted 70 hides to landing.

8 SEPTEMBER 1934 — SATURDAY
Took a load of salt across to the camp; this is the last of it.
Stopped camp shooting. I fear something must have
happened to the *Chantress* as it should have been here on the
3rd. I will wait a few days longer before going into Darwin.

10 SEPTEMBER 1934 — MONDAY
Went over to the camp this morning and put all the blacks
on bush tucker. I made a couple of harpoons and put two
boys onto catching alligators. I cut the tobacco issue down.
Will shift back to main camp tomorrow and go into Darwin
in a day or so to find out what has happened to the *Chantress*.

11 SEPTEMBER 1934 — TUESDAY
Packed up and went back to main camp. Max Freer came
across to see me. Decided to send Wallaby across to
Marrakai Station with a letter to Hazel Gaden, who is part
owner of *Chantress*.

12 SEPTEMBER 1934 — WEDNESDAY
Started Wallaby across to Marrakai with instructions to
walk day and night. Borrowed some more rations off Max
Freer. Returned to camp. Boys very unsettled likely to go
any crack of the whip.

13 SEPTEMBER 1934 — THURSDAY
This morning started two boys catching 'gators. Self and
Peter mustering horses round near landing and met boat,
which had just come up on the morning tide. Sent back to
camp for team horses. Boat discharged 3 tons of salt and ½
ton of rations. Carted all the rations over to camp and
returned to landing and camped. Sent over for alligator men
to come back.

20 SEPTEMBER 1934 — THURSDAY
Tubby is a good shooting horse, but not quite strong enough
for the long gallops on the plains. Domestic upheaval —
Peter, who has been very henpecked, gave his lubra, Rosie, a
good hiding.

24 SEPTEMBER 1934 — MONDAY
Foot shooter laid up with bad foot owing to horse walking
on him. Self and Government foot shooting. Packhorse
boys got lost in the jungle and spoilt day's shooting.

2 OCTOBER 1934 — TUESDAY
Shooting across where I lost Rifle. Sent Wallaby to track
horse up but never found it. Nine hides. Two boys turned up
from Marrakai (Gaden's camp) where they have just finished
the season's shoot having got two thousand hides since the
middle of May.

5 OCTOBER 1934 — FRIDAY
Self shooting again. Tried Dollar out for shooting horse and
went very well. Knocked six hefty bulls off him. Intended
selling him when I got back to Pine Creek, but if he doesn't
get gun-shy £25 won't buy him.

6 OCTOBER 1934 — SATURDAY
Started Government and his lubra, Joe and Wallaby across to
Ban Yan Point to catch alligators. Packed a bag of salt and
rations and camped there for the first night myself to give

them a start. Owing to strong N.W. winds during day, can only catch them early morning.

7 OCTOBER 1934 — SUNDAY
Got 3 alligators and five buffalo.

8 OCTOBER 1934 — MONDAY
There was a fight in the camp last night between Buckley and Joe (the eternal triangle). Just got down there in time to take their spears off them and made them fight fists 'finger fight'. This resulted in a win for Buckley, he's got three lubras now. They will probably finish it in the bush with spears after we knock off and one of them will get a passage off this planet! Two alligators and seven buffalo.

9 OCTOBER 1934 — TUESDAY
Buckley's two lubras belted hell out of him last night and sent his latest prize bush. Buckley back to square one (or two?).

18 OCTOBER 1934 — THURSDAY
To landing with 29 hides and fetched two bags of salt back to camp. Boys went out and got 11 hides, which completes the tally. Everyone is very glad it's finished. Horses all want a spell. Wounded bull charged the packhorses today and caught Bangle, according to the boys. I think her stifle is broken.

24 OCTOBER 1934 — WEDNESDAY
Mustering the plant horses all day. Now we have stopped shooting they are scattering about Hell West and Crooked. Got them all together except two.

27 OCTOBER 1934 — SATURDAY
Venture arrived this morning, which is just as well as Max was talking about going to Darwin by canoe because they had run out of rations. Heavy rain after dinner. Got some mail and £15 in notes.

4 NOVEMBER 1934 — SUNDAY
Chantress arrived on tonight's tide.

5 NOVEMBER 1934 — MONDAY
Went over to landing with dray to get supplies off the
Chantress. I gave all the natives their 'pay off', amid much
excitement. Sent Billy over to alligator camp for the rest of
the alligator hides. He returned at sundown with seven,
making a total of 52. *Chantress* took on board 140 hides.

14 NOVEMBER 1934 — WEDNESDAY
Decided to go today.

20 NOVEMBER 1934 — TUESDAY
Another good storm. Wet season settling in.

27 NOVEMBER 1934 — TUESDAY
Arrived at Goodparla Station and camped Gerowie Creek
with Monty Sullivan, who is recognised as one of the best
horsemen in Australia. Monty is part owner of Goodparla.

29 NOVEMBER 1934 — THURSDAY
Pine Creek. All the old mines (gold) are starting up again
and there are hundreds of men here. Mines previously closed
down are now payable owing to modern machinery and the
increased price of gold.

5 DECEMBER 1934 — WEDNESDAY
Pine Creek. Tommy Sullivan shot Jack Dixon last night.
Sullivan was previously foreman at Umalbar.

KAPALGA
NORTHERN TERRITORY

14 DECEMBER 1934

Dear Mum

Received several letters from you and haven't had much of a chance to write.

When I returned to my camp from Darwin I had very few horses left. Some damned disease had got among them and all my good horses died, including most of my good harness horses. I had 11 harness horses last year. This year I only had two of them left. I had some young colts and unbroken stuff and managed to muster about 20 head, but they were mostly poor. I decided to give them all a month's spell on good grass and go over to Marrakai and get some donkeys and horses off Hazel Gaden, a friend of mine, who was buffalo shooting. He often works my horses when he is short and I often work his.

To cut a long story short, I started shooting on August 4 and had agreed to have 200 hides at the landing by the end of the month for the lugger *Chantress*, which was to deliver to me three more tons of salt and another load of rations. Anyhow, the lugger never turned up until about the 13th and I was practically out of everything. The camp was hung up for about a fortnight and I was giving my famous imitation of a lunatic at large, but as a matter of fact, I thought the boat had sunk.

I had a go at the alligators this year and hoped to get a good few, but owing to all the delays I couldn't get at them properly. I sent 51 skins away. The work isn't so hard and I don't require such a large camp, so the running expenses aren't a quarter so high.

Just at present there is a mining boom on here and all the old gold mines have been restarted. Owing to the high price of gold and modern machinery, the gold mines are a payable proposition.

I am going out to a mine about 30 miles from Pine Creek to do a bit of butchering for them. Also, I am going to do all their packhorse work in the wet season, which is now overdue. As soon as it starts to rain, all roads will be impassable for motor trucks and I will be packing rations out to them with my packhorses.

I am going to try to get hold of a butchering business either here or at Gove Hill, another mining centre about 40 miles away.

I haven't heard from Uncle Tom for years. I hope I haven't missed some mail as I know I miss a lot of local letters, which is on account of having no service and having to get it out by anybody that comes along.

I hope you have had a happy Christmas. I shall be working hard putting up a house (bark) and a stockyard on Evelyn Creek close to Eureka Mine.

Love to everybody, your loving son
Tom

18 DECEMBER 1934 — TUESDAY

I have decided to go to Evelyn and butcher for Eureka Mine and other prospectors, for the duration of the wet season. I let the boy Peter go for spell and put two more boys on.

20 DECEMBER 1934 — THURSDAY

Left Pine Creek with enough rations to last a week. The rest of the stuff to come out later in a motor lorry. Camped at Esmeralda.

28 DECEMBER 1934 — FRIDAY

Cutting timber for yard, beef house and boys' house.

29 DECEMBER 1934 — SATURDAY

Went down the river to where the North Australian Exploration Company is mining and got a standing order for 52 pounds of beef per week.

31 DECEMBER 1934 — MONDAY

Sent boys down the river to strip paperbark for a house for themselves.

1935

1 JANUARY 1935 — TUESDAY
Boys are still stripping bark. Made arrangements for North
Australian Exploration Co. to cart it up to my camp in their
lorry. Driest January ever experienced by all hands in this
district; this time last year water and bog was everywhere.

21 JANUARY 1935 — MONDAY
Started to break in horses to saddle. Have quite a lot of
horses that are only broken in to carry hides. Started on
Rapid and tackled him this morning. It looks as though he
will be a bad buckjumper. Still dry.

23 JANUARY 1935 — WEDNESDAY
Tackled Biddy and Vision this morning and rode Sligo and
Rapid. Killed after dinner. The boy Peter while coming
home in the dark after delivering Eureka beef had his horse
bolt and got a bad fall in timber.

Required for Shooting Camp
Carborundum stone   Billy cans
Dray saddle   .303 magazines (2)
Plates   Bolts — fine copper wire (5/8 × 4)
Table knives   Trigger guard for shot gun

Top left: Tom Cole just before leaving England, aged 17 years.

Top right: A 'flying camp' in scrub country, two canvas tent-flys over saplings.

Bottom: Carting stores and salt back to the camp.

Top: Branding at Lake Nash Station.

Centre: Wildman River.

Bottom: Spearing dugong at George Hunter's station, Woolner, near Adelaide River. The native canoe has been hewn out of a solid log.

Top left: Stockmen at Burnside Station in the Northern Territory.

Top right: Fred Morris with a recently killed crocodile.

Bottom left: Two bulls shot in dense scrub, which was difficult country to gallop through.

Bottom right: A wounded buffalo with a broken back; the shot has paralysed its hindquarters. Tom was riding his grey mare, Cloud, when he shot this bull. The hide would have weighed one hundred pounds or more.

Top: Skinning buffalo on the Wildman plains. The plains make perfect riding country when the water dries off; it's like a racecourse, it's covered in couch grass.

Centre: Shooters and packhorses walking through the dry bed of the West Alligator River. Only a series of waterholes remain, and the river bed is covered in couch grass.

Bottom: West Alligator River.

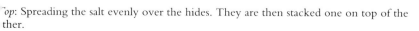

Top: Spreading the salt evenly over the hides. They are then stacked one on top of the other.

Centre: Yorky Billy skinning a buffalo.

Bottom: A camp at Gypsy Spring.

Top left: Woman and child. The women did most of the salting, curing and drying of the buffalo hides in the shooting camps.

Top right: Old Government (Manggargil) making a paperbark raft at Alec's Hole, Northern Territory.

Bottom: The first police camp set up at Tennant Creek in 1933.

Top: Buffalo hides stacked on the bank of the South Alligator River waiting for the *Maroubra*.

Bottom: Shooters with a dead buffalo on the West Alligator River. Ring is mounted, Government (Manggargil) is seated on the hide, and the other fellow is Paddy.

Top: Loading buffalo hides at Wildman River. Hazel Gaden is on the truck.

Bottom: Unloading sacks of salt from the *Chantress* at Kapalga landing, South Alligator River.

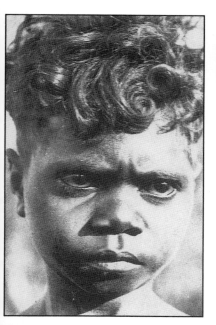

Top left: Aboriginal boy.

Top right: Mary, Yorky Billy's wife, washing mud and dirt off the skins before they are salted and dried.

Bottom: Buffalo shooter Fred Hardy, at his station Mt Bundey, Adelaide River.

Top: A visiting truck at a buffalo camp on the Wildman River.

Bottom: Tom Cole on his favourite shooting mare, Trinket, with a wounded bull in the foreground.

Top: The *Maroubra* at Sampan Creek between the Wildman and Mary Rivers.

Bottom: Aboriginal boys crossing the East Alligator River on barrels. They were going to Oenpelli mission 40 miles away to radio for a doctor – Jack Gaden was seriously ill.

Top: Tom Cole, Hazel Gaden and Fred Morris at Gypsy Spring near Kapalga, 1936. In the foreground are metal water bags for the dry season.

Bottom: Tom Cole standing (right) with a visitor to his camp, George Taylor, editor of the Melbourne *Sun*, standing (left) and Harry Stotts.

Top left: In the process of building a yard and a shed for the truck at Ingarrabba Station. Behind the men bringing in a wild pig is the framework for the gates. A pack saddle is in the foreground.

Top right: Banana Creek, a tributary of the Wildman River.

Bottom: Final drying of hides on some racks.

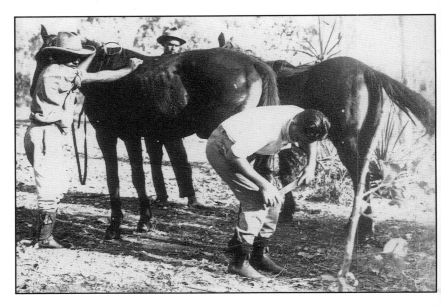

Top: George Stevens, shoeing the shooting horses.

Bottom: Tom Cole shooting a wounded bull.

Top: Spearing fish on the Wildman River.

Bottom: Tom Cole's donkeys outside Pine Creek railway station.

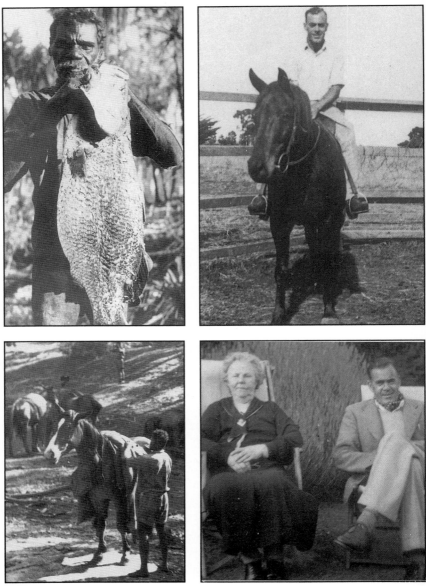

Top left: Old Government with a barramundi, West Alligator River.

Top right: Tom Cole on a newly broken colt.

Bottom left: Unloading hides at the Banana Creek buffalo camp after a day's shooting. The hides are first of all washed in water.

Bottom right: Tom Cole visiting his mother for the first time in England 25 years after he had left.

19 APRIL 1935 — FRIDAY
Packed up and went into Pine Creek to catch train down to
Darwin on Monday. Took six horses and two packs,
together with horses Eagle and Dollar for a race meeting to
be held tomorrow.

20 APRIL 1935 — SATURDAY
Started Eagle and Dollar in the Flying Handicap. I rode
Eagle and won after a close finish. I started him in another
race but ran fourth.

21 APRIL 1935 — SUNDAY
Put on a lad named Joe from the blacks' camp here and will
take him out buffalo shooting and try and make a horseman
of him. He's a likely looking lad.

23 APRIL 1935 — TUESDAY
Darwin. Put orders into Jolly's for rations and 8 tons of salt.
Took a contract for 300 hides, making 800 orders in all.

11 MAY 1935 — SATURDAY
Packed up and went as far as the Mary River. Camped with
Yorky Mick and Paddy Bennet, a couple of prospectors. The
former is going into Pine Creek and the latter out to the
Alligator River.

12 MAY 1935 — SUNDAY
Goodparla Station. I have a good few horses running around
here and will put in a couple of days of mustering.

13 MAY 1935 — MONDAY
Out with Monty Sullivan mustering the big paddock. Got
five horses of mine. Picked up one camp boy here
(Government) in a very bad way. Another black fellow has
stolen his lubra.

15 MAY 1935 — WEDNESDAY
Put in a day handling the colts I got off Monty yesterday.
Will try and get away tomorrow. Should be leaving here
with 27 head of horses, five packs, five riding saddles, all in
first class order. With the horses I left down the Wildman I
should have about 40 head of good workers.

16 MAY 1935 — THURSDAY
Left Goodparla after dinner and camped at Nine Mile Yard
— a mob of bush blacks following behind — 27 horses in
hand.

22 MAY 1935 — WEDNESDAY
Left this morning. Have to get around some bad swamps.
Camped in the scrub after making some big westerly
deviations. Very bad horse camp — no grass and very bad
water. Expect there will be horses away tomorrow morning.
Hobbled everything short. Have no idea how far we are
from Kapalga. Neither the boys nor myself know this
country.

23 MAY 1935 — THURSDAY
Horses mustered and we are six short this morning, so were
held up for a couple of hours while boys tracked them. A
pack horse knocked up so pulled up for dinner earlier than I
intended, to let him have a spell. After dinner went on
again. About four o'clock came into some country that
appeared familiar so sent a boy up a tall tree and he could
see the Ingarrabba hills and the Kapalga jungle so we went
on again with fresh heart and got to Kapalga at dusk.

24 MAY 1935 — FRIDAY
Kapalga — overgrown with hoarhound and undergrowth —
put two boys onto cutting a track to the landing. I took two
boys and all the horses out onto good grass on the plain,
about three miles out.

26 MAY 1935 — SUNDAY
Maroubra arrived on this morning's tide — discharged 80
sacks of salt, 20 sacks of flour, six sacks of sugar, two cases
of cartridges, 13 cases of sundries, three rifles, four sacks of
oats and eight bales of fodder — left on same tide.

4 JUNE 1935 — TUESDAY
Crossed the dray over the swamp and left it there.
Tomorrow will start to cart all the salt and some rations to
lower West Alligator Crossing. Will probably take me four
days.

15 JUNE 1935 — SATURDAY
Took dray and buckboard across to West Alligator Crossing
for salt. Had a lot of trouble on the road clearing fallen
timber. Started to clear a path through the grass and
bulrushes to get across the swamp. Cleared about half way.
Made a pontoon with six drums. Leeches very bad.

16 JUNE 1935 — SUNDAY
Finished clearing path for pontoon and crossed a ton of salt.

17 JUNE 1935 — MONDAY
Tried to put horse called Blossom into harness this morning
and the team bolted. Managed to stop them. As the brake is
a bit weak I decided to postpone her education. Returned to
camp with only four horses in the dray.

19 JUNE 1935 — WEDNESDAY
Got away with a good start and got to Banana Creek for
dinner; rigged a camp, ran up a horse yard and shot four
buffalo alongside the camp — a very good day's work. Start
shooting tomorrow.

20 JUNE 1935 — THURSDAY
Fifteen head of horses cleared off back to the Wildman last
night. Clary and Jack tracked them back and it was eleven

o'clock before I got a start. Gave Clary a rifle and put him
up on Dollar and let him shoot a buffalo. He may make a
good horse-back shooter. Self shot six, could have got a lot
more only none of these boys are experienced skinners and
we had our hands full.

22 JUNE 1935 — SATURDAY
Went out foot shooting in the jungle today. Packhorses went
bush and didn't turn up till after dinner, to where I was
waiting with two bulls down. The boys with the packhorses
had numerous excuses, 'I bin think . . .'

23 JUNE 1935 — SUNDAY
Went up the creek horseback shooting. Horse called
Thunder seems to be getting gun-shy. He may get over it or
he may get worse. Tomorrow will decide. Got thrown and
trampled on and seven hides.

24 JUNE 1935 — MONDAY
Thunder a washout as far as shooting horse. Got ten hides,
would have got more if the horse had gone up to the
buffaloes. Clary shot six.

28 JUNE 1935 — FRIDAY
Rained pretty well all night, blankets all wet. Very cold.
Decided not to go out today. Natives all getting bark and
building elaborate humpies, so I expect the rain will clear.

6 JULY 1935 — SATURDAY
Went down the plains this morning and got horses, Trinket,
Dozey, Vision and Trixie. Left again after dinner and went
back to Wildman. Crossed the West Alligator River in the
dark and got the pack bags with my swag, all the tucker and
three dozen boxes of matches, full of water and I didn't
know until I got to the Wildman about midnight.

10 JULY 1935 — WEDNESDAY
The second hundred aren't going to be too easy. Rode a long
way today and got back to camp late at night with eight hides.

11 JULY 1935 — THURSDAY
Poor day today — only four hides. Horses are giving a lot of
trouble. A boy was away all day tracking horses that had
cleared back to Wildman. Tragedy in the blacks' camp —
one of their dogs picked up a dingo bait and was gathered
unto his father.

15 JULY 1935 — MONDAY
Boy Peter returned to camp with the harness horses and a
letter from Dave written with charcoal on a board saying
buggy wheel all broken and a lot more details which I
couldn't understand. From what boy says I think we will
pretty well have to make a new wheel.

17 JULY 1935 — WEDNESDAY
Shifted camp across to Spring Camp. Will take a week to fix
the buckboard wheel. Will have to practically make a new
wheel.

21 JULY 1935 — SUNDAY
Shot up by the Wildman river and got seven hides. I saw a
lot of smoke signals from blacks going across from Wildman
to Flying Fox. I sent Jack up to try and intercept them but he
failed to do so.

24 JULY 1935 — WEDNESDAY
Dave nearly finished the wheel. Has made all the spokes (12)
and five felloes using one felloe from old wheel. Couldn't
use any spokes though as they were all broken.

9 AUGUST 1935 — FRIDAY
Out early this morning to skin the six buffalo left from
yesterday. Shot one more and returned early to camp to

repair a riding saddle. Have 255 hides and will start carting
tomorrow. Wanted to get 350 for this boat. Only 100 out in
my calculation!

19 AUGUST 1935 — MONDAY
Cut and carted timber and built a jetty for *Maroubra*.

22 AUGUST 1935 — THURSDAY
No boat.

26 AUGUST 1935 — MONDAY
Decided to return to main camp as tucker is getting short.
Curse all boats. I met a boy from Gaden's along the road;
Gaden is at my camp on his way to shoot in Kapalga
country. He has a plant of horses, donkey team and motor
lorry.

1 SEPTEMBER 1935 — SUNDAY
Shot across to Flying Fox and struck a patch of buffalo —
got 11. Will shift over to the crossing tomorrow and camp
for a few days, where there is half a ton of salt that I can
use.

16 SEPTEMBER 1935 — MONDAY
All the buffalo here very poor condition. Beef question very
serious. Counting lubras and kids there are seventeen blacks
to be fed and they get away with a good deal of tucker. One
boy and some lubras stripping bark.

17 SEPTEMBER 1935 — TUESDAY
Rosie, Peter's lubra, has been sick with a pain in the right
side since the middle of last month. I have come to the
conclusion that she has appendicitis or at any rate needs
medical attention as she seems to be getting worse. Will go
over to Gaden's camp tomorrow and try and get one of them
to run her and Peter into the Arnhem Land Mine, from
where they should be able to get into Pine Creek.

18 SEPTEMBER 1935 — WEDNESDAY
Instructed boys to carry on shooting. Put Rosie in the dray
and told Peter to fetch her back to the Spring Camp. Started
for Spring Camp. Got about a mile along the road and met
old man Peter with a letter from Dave saying Sawdy on his
way to Darwin for rations. Will pass within a mile of this
camp. Turned dray back. Waited for car, fetched it into
camp, put Rosie and family aboard for hospital.

1 OCTOBER 1935 — TUESDAY
Returned to camp. Three boys left while I was away
(Bumble, Joe and Toby). Got a boy out of the bush camp and
gave him a start. He is also named Toby. He worked for me
once before on the prospecting trip in '33.

2 OCTOBER 1935 — WEDNESDAY
Got in to camp and no Topsy. Topsy (Ring's lubra) has
presumably followed Bumble with another young girl from
the camp. Ring breathing fire. There'll be blood on the
moon when Ring and Bumble meet.

3 OCTOBER 1935 — THURSDAY
Ring left this morning to track Topsy and Bumble. Hope he
won't be away very long as he is the best boy I have and a
very good horseback shooter. Shorthanded now, only three
boys today, Jack who was away looking for missing horses
and Toby and Clary.

4 OCTOBER 1935 — FRIDAY
Decided to shift back to Red Rock for a week, to give the
plains here a chance to fill up again. Will have to shoot very
carefully to get 800 hides. If I shoot at one camp too much,
the buffalo won't come back. I stand a good chance of
getting my contracts.

7 OCTOBER 1935 — MONDAY
Supposed to be a big mob of blackfellows coming down the
river. I suppose they will be here in hundreds when it's time
to knock off shooting. Very shorthanded.

9 OCTOBER 1935 — WEDNESDAY
Horse called Cricket gave his famous imitation of a cyclone
this morning and threw Clary and jumped on his ribs and put
him out of action for a while. Another man short.

12 OCTOBER 1935 — SATURDAY
Put 14 hides on the dray and shifted back to Spring Camp.
Left old Peter and his spouse to dry out the rest of the hides.
No word back from Gaden, so as there is no salt took seven
packhorses after supper and started to Kapalga. Got to the
crossing (seven miles), about 11 o'clock and found Gaden and
Sawdy. Gaden with salt on and Sawdy bogged to the
radiator cap. Put in the rest of the night pulling him out.

13 OCTOBER 1935 — SUNDAY
Gaden and self together fixed front spring. Took salt to
Spring Camp. Went on to Red Rock and loaded 74 hides and
started back when the moon rose, without lights.

14 OCTOBER 1935 — MONDAY
By day light this morning, we had come seven miles —
made five fan belts, mended two punctures, unloaded and
reloaded three times, carried water for radiator over
distances varying from 200 yards to two miles — about the
only thing we didn't do was sleep. At sunrise we threw off
30 hides owing to differential grinding — two miles further,
we unloaded the rest, two miles from the Spring Camp, the
pinion went and we walked in. Sent a boy to Sawdy's camp
on West Alligator River and he came in utility truck, took a
small load of my hides and Jack Gaden back to his camp.
Retired slightly exhausted.

15 OCTOBER 1935 — TUESDAY
Didn't get away from camp this morning until ten o'clock
owing to horses clearing out down the plain. Had to go five
miles before we struck buffalo and knocked 17 down.
Managed to get them skinned before sundown by cutting out
dinner and got back to camp at half past nine. Had supper
washed and salted hides and turned in at ten past twelve.
Very romantic life, this buffalo shooting.

19 OCTOBER 1935 — SATURDAY
Took a load of hides from Spring Camp to crossing. Went
with Sawdy to Kapalga with a load and got a puncture at
Kapalga and had to walk back for a spare tube. Sent boys
back to Red Rock with dray for hides.

20 OCTOBER 1935 — SUNDAY
Ted Sawdy got his truck back and went up and shifted his
camp down to here. Hell of a mob here now and a lot of
bush blacks hanging around. Shod horse called Nigger and
got kicked.

21 OCTOBER 1935 — MONDAY
Nigger swerved into a tree when a bull charged and I got a
black shin out of it. Lame in both legs now. Buffalo flies
very bad and tormenting horses. Heat almost unbearable,
storms working up. Would like to knock off, want 180 hides
to complete contracts. Have 620 shot.

22 OCTOBER 1935 — TUESDAY
Gave Ring a packhorse and a couple of saddle horses and let
him go up to Bamboo Creek to try and find his lubra.

25 OCTOBER 1935 — FRIDAY
Ring returned from Bamboo Creek without his lubra.
Maroubra arrived on tonight's tide. There are no rations for
either Gaden or myself — Position serious — I will have to
go into Pine Creek as quickly as I can. *Maroubra* — loaded

my hides on by midnight — 366. Something is wrong in
Darwin — lots of goods ordered by me from South should
have been here. I have received advice that my goods were
landed in Darwin.

26 OCTOBER 1935 — SATURDAY
Maroubra — loaded Gaden's hides and left on this morning's
tide. Dave went with her into Darwin. Bought Gaden's
motor lorry this morning. Gaden will get a new pinion and
radiator and try and get her into the telegraph line for me, if
the wet doesn't set in and stop him.

28 OCTOBER 1935 — MONDAY
Packed things up in the bark humpies here and started to
build a humpy over the motor lorry. Put 17 horses onto the
Wildman Plains — will leave them here for the wet. Taking
13 horses to Pine Creek.

29 OCTOBER 1935 — TUESDAY
Gaden went through this morning with Sawdy — on their
way to Darwin for rations. Sold Gaden four horses. Finished
building the humpy over the lorry and jacked it up. Got
away after dinner.

DARWIN
NORTHERN TERRITORY
15 NOVEMBER 1935
Dear Mum
Have just returned to civilization after the shooting. Have
done fairly well, having shot 250 from September to October.
The price of buffalo hides, however, has dropped from 5½
pence to 3½ pence per pound which is pretty considerable.
      I contracted with a firm of buyers to supply 200 and got 50
over my contract. I am negotiating at present to try and place
the remaining 50 at a decent price. The fall in prices doesn't

affect me for 200 hides, but of course they aren't keen on taking the other 50.

I am in Darwin at present, but am going back to the Alligator River next Sunday to load my hides and fetch them in. Just at present, I am very busy and am hurrying to catch the aerial mail, which leaves shortly. I know you will be anxious to hear from me.

I will write you another long letter later, giving you some of the details of the shoot and I will send you some photographs.

With fondest love, your loving son

PINE CREEK
NORTHERN TERRITORY

12 DECEMBER 1935

Dear Mum

It seems a long time to me since I wrote to you and I suppose longer to you. I received several of your letters all at once when I was shooting. The boat that brought them went straight back, so I couldn't have replied to them even if I had had the time.

I noticed that you are expecting me to come home, but this is definitely off for several reasons, the principal being that I haven't the necessary money. Also, I don't think it would be wise while the exchange rate is standing at 25 per cent as I can hardly afford to lose £25 in the £100.

I have finished shooting for this season and am, as usual, at a dead end for the wet season, which is just about on us. I did not do as well as I should have but nevertheless it was the best year I've had.

I have bought a 30 cwt truck and also purchased Kapalga Station, which adjoins my present holding. I have just returned from Darwin, having had the transfers made. Kapalga is a very useful buffalo shooting proposition and I am looking forward to a good season next year. There is every indication of a rise in hides and if I can get 5½ pence per pound I can make £1000 next year. I don't anticipate any difficulty getting 1000 hides.

I will have to put a lot back into the place as there are conditions attached to holding country. I have it under what is known as a Grazing Licence and the rent is 1 shilling per square mile, plus £1 licence fee for each area. Kapalga being one area (200 square miles) and what I call the Wildman Block (my original holding) the other (300 square miles), in total I hold 500 square miles. I held two other blocks, but threw them up in 1933 and wanted to take them up again in '35 (this year). But the Lands Department wouldn't grant me the country unless I paid the rent on it for '34, and this I refused to do as I didn't occupy it. These grazing licences are not a very secure tenure. They can be converted into pastoral leases and thrown open, and the previous holder does not necessarily get preference when applications are considered. I have, however applied to the Lands Department for permission to erect £1000 worth of improvements and then if the country is thrown open to pastoral leasing, it is very improbable that anyone would pay for that much when there is so much crown land available merely by paying the rent.

I shot 620 hides this year, I expect you remember my contracts were for 800. I would have easily got them but the local merchants 'forgot' to ship my last order for rations by the *Maroubra*, the coastal vessel that carted my loading from Darwin and hides back. The consequence was that I had to knock off shooting in October, 180 hides short on my contracts. My last day's shooting was 17 and I stopped shooting about 12th. I could have got my contracts in another fortnight.

However things could have been worse. I cleared about £300 but haven't got much now. I have three or four months to put in and I'm not too sure what I'll be doing, but probably running brumbies (wild horses) and breaking in. It will be about a month before the wet sets in properly and then, of course, it is impossible to do anything. Water and bog are everywhere. In the wet, grass is long and rank and horses don't do too well, so I generally repair gear and get everything shipshape for the shooting season.

Freddy Morris, my friend, is going to send you some more

photos. I don't know when as he is pretty hard to get at these days as a girl has the Indian sign on him. I stayed with him last time I was in Darwin, but didn't see much of him and as a matter of fact put in most of my time at the Qantas Empire Airways quarters. I was there when Jim Broadbent arrived from England and he told us that Kingsford Smith passed him over the Persian Gulf. He was probably the last one to see his plane. We were more than disappointed when Smithy didn't turn up. They all seem to go the same way.

Now I have the Kapalga holding, I intend forming a station and putting cattle on it. I will probably put 100 breeders on next August if hides are a good price.

I had a letter from Dora the other day and was pleased to hear from her, but I haven't heard from Uncle Tom for years. I'll drop him a line and ask him if he's retired from letter writing, too.

I have a camera now and so will be able to send you some photos next year. I am enclosing a few that a friend of mine took who came out on the *Maroubra* to see me before he went away for holidays. It was Jack Kepert, the pearler, and while he was away from Darwin on this trip his number one diver died of diver's paralysis, a disease which attacks divers while below after shell. The Darwin pearlers lost a lot of divers this year. One diver was bitten by a sea snake on the wrist, the only portion of a diver that is not protected with a heavy rubber suit. These snakes, which are numerous in the tropic seas, are the most venomous snakes in the world.

Speaking, or rather writing of snakes, recently I was coming from Goodparla Station with a packhorse plant and I camped at a spring 12 miles from Pine Creek, known for some obscure reason as the Nine Mile Spring. Anyhow, I struck the Esmeralda mustering plant and young Fred Stevens, the station owner's son, was in charge. We laid our swags out beside the spring alongside one another and were yarning away. The night was a bright moonlight almost like day.

About half past nine or ten, Fred gave a blood curdling yell and broke all existing records for the high jump, long jump and the 100 yards dash. I didn't know whether it was a ghost or hostile blacks. Looking over to his swag I could see coiled up and gleaming in the bright moonlight a snake fully seven feet long. Fred's yell soon brought the boys down from their camp and with a stick they quickly killed it. We found it to be a Darwin Brown, one of the deadliest snakes in the world.

When I saw it first, it was coiled up on Fred's camp sheet and goodness knows how long it had been there. Fred said his attention was first drawn to it when he felt something touch him. He looked to see what it was and then he travelled!

I am sending this letter aerial mail and hope you receive it for Christmas. I may not get any mail for a long time. I don't know exactly where I'll be, but I'll try and get my Christmas mail.

I hope you all have a happy Christmas and a bright New Year. My love to you all.

Your loving son
P.S. Am sending photos by ordinary mail as it would make this letter too heavy and cost too much by aerial.

1936

30 MARCH 1936 — MONDAY
Left Dorisvale with 27 head of fat horses. Went to Lewin Springs Station and will wait for Jimmy Hart. I have to muster the horse paddock for some of my horses that I left here during the wet.

1 APRIL 1936 — WEDNESDAY
Went to Rutherven Station, Dick Guild's place — I have some more horses to pick up here. Dick not at home but will be back in a few days. I will leave most of the horses in the paddock. I will also leave a few horses and a couple of packs with Jack Hore and get him to meet the train when I come back from Darwin.

2 APRIL 1936 — THURSDAY
Rode across to Jack Hore's farm on the Edith River, 7 miles from the siding.

3 APRIL 1936 — FRIDAY
Rode to the siding and sent my saddle and packhorses back to Jack Hore's with boy and caught the train. Train only two hours late today, must be after some international record. Got to Pine Creek an hour early without blowing up! Stay the night here.

4 APRIL 1936 — SATURDAY
Went on to Darwin this morning, arrived 4 p.m.

6 APRIL 1936 — MONDAY
Darwin. Arranged to supply Northern Agency with 500
hides at 5 pence per lb.

7 APRIL 1936 — TUESDAY
Made up an order for goods required for coming season and
sent it to Sydney by airmail. Saw Cecil Hall, skipper of the
Maroubra, about coming out with my loading about the end
of May and taking my hides in for the rest of the season.

8 APRIL 1936 — WEDNESDAY
Left Darwin by train. Stayed the night in Pine Creek.

9 APRIL 1936 — THURSDAY
Edith River. Dick Guild back. Met me at the siding.

10 APRIL 1936 — FRIDAY
Straightening up the plant — making hobble straps — going
over the gear — greasing saddles and harness. Got one of my
camp boys (Clary).

13 APRIL 1936 — MONDAY
Mustered Horseshoe Creek for some of my horses but only
got two — King and Cricket.

18 APRIL 1936 — SATURDAY
Mustering horses today and a horse fell with me. Only
middling.

19 APRIL 1936 — SUNDAY
Dick rode away early this morning to Katherine (26 miles)
and is getting a car to fetch me into hospital. The car arrived
at sundown — road in shocking state — hospital 11 p.m.

KATHERINE HOSPITAL
NORTH AUSTRALIA

27 APRIL 1936

Dear Uncle

I expect you will be surprised to get a letter from me from the above address, but as a matter of fact I've had a bit of bad luck. A horse fell with me while horse mustering on the Edith River and I got hurt a bit. I have been in here eight days now. There is no doctor here, but they sent one down from Darwin (200 miles away) to have a look at me a few days ago. He reckons that I will be under treatment for at least another six weeks. My left leg has been badly hurt and an old injury in the ankle joint is affected. I don't get much sleep except when they give me a shot of morphine and they are pretty lousy with it. It's worse than getting blood from a stone.

From what I can make out, there is something wrong with the bone. The doctor blinded me with science for half an hour and I still know nothing.

It's come at a pretty bad time for me as I was just off to start shooting. I had been to Darwin and contracted to shoot 500 hides. The firm that was buying them were backing me for supplies up to £200 and there is £180 worth of stuff on the next Sydney boat. I've had to sub-let that contract and won't make anything out of it.

Pretty mournful turnout, isn't it? Anyhow, it is the devil. This year would have put me on velvet and now I see everything I've slaved for slipping away. If I could only move or get temporarily patched up I'd take a chance and get down, but I can't move, I'm crippled.

Anyhow, what all this is leading up to is cash. Can you cable me ten or fifteen pounds? I'm sorry to have to ask for it and never intended doing so, but I never expected to be caught like this. I don't know when I can repay it, but if luck breaks my way you should get it back this year.

When I get a bit better I think they are going to shift me to Darwin, but if they can treat me here I don't want to go.

Darwin hospital is full of dying patients, generally. As I'm the only one here, I get well looked after and, if necessary, they can always get the doctor down on the plane. He is coming down in a few days to give me the once over again.

The nurses are very good, although they tell me I'm the world's worst patient.

Well, Uncle, It's taken me two days to write this letter and I'm just about knocked up, so will say goodbye. I've answered your other letter and Xmas card, but you won't get it for a while, it's gone ordinary mail.

Please don't tell Mum about this as she'll worry like the Devil and I'm quite all right. I've got a constitution like a horse and I'll soon be in the saddle again knocking down buffalo in a couple of months.

Love to all, your sincere nephew

HOSPITAL
KATHERINE
NORTH AUSTRALIA

26 MAY 1936

Dear Mum

Haven't heard from you for ages and ages, so I s'pose your letters have been going astray somewhere. One of these days I'll get a wad of mail that has been roaming around the Northern Territory somewhere, although, since I've settled down on the coast, the post office fellows aren't too bad.

As you will see by my present address I'm undergoing a rest cure and at not a bad place either. We have a good cook and good nurse. We average about two patients, although I'm on my own a lot and get all the attention.

My first comrade only lasted about three days and they planted him, but I've got another mate now and I think he'll be hard to kill off. I've been in here five weeks, which seems a long time but it's longer than that.

A fool of a horse fell with me when I was mustering horses

on the Edith River, just as I was about to start down to my buffalo camp. My foot got twisted up a bit, but she's going pretty good now and I'll be out by hook or by crook by the middle of June.

It caught me at a very bad time — just as I was starting the season — every penny I had, and a lot more I didn't have, was sunk into the shooting. The price of hides was right up and I was going to make a big punch and reckoned I was as good as on my feet, and bang goes everything.

I had signed up to deliver 500 hides in Darwin by the end of August. Of course, had to sub-let that contract. I could see I couldn't get out of here and get down on the job and knock 500 over and deliver them in that time.

Anyhow, my friend Freddy Morris who was with me before is coming down again to get a bit of shooting and he is leaving Darwin June 12th and is going to pick me up in Pine Creek. I'm sure to be out by then. We are going to try to get down to my camp in his car. Of course there are no roads and the distance is something under 200 miles, but I think we can manage. He has a big heavy touring car, which can stand a few knocks.

I wrote to Uncle Tom for the loan of a few quid to see me out of a hole and I got £25 cabled to me from Worthing. No name and no address, so I don't know who to thank for it; anyhow, I suppose you will know who it is and I want to thank them. I hope to be able to repay it very soon but will have to get some hides shot first.

Now don't you get worrying about me, I'm fine and improving so fast I can't catch up myself. I only weigh 9 stone but that's good for the horses as they carry a light weight better. Anyhow, I bet I'm ten stone next week.

I think I've got a bone (only a small one) broken or it may be only bruised. There's something wrong with a cartilage, which may take a while to get properly right but isn't serious. A small abscess on the ankle or joint or thereabouts completes the list. It's nothing much — I've just got to rest up that's all — simple. My foot isn't quite straight, but it's sure to be all right later because they have a good splint on it and it's just got to grow straight — it's got no option. The only thing that annoys me is that I'm here instead of shooting; it's just a bit tough for me. Anyhow I'll be out by the middle of June and then all you'll see of me for four months will be a cloud of dust. I'll be shooting by July for sure, I think.

I've got a great plant his year. I've built it up during the last wet and now have 60 working horses and a good 30 cwt motor lorry and extra country. Everything is right up to the knocker and, although I won't make quite as much as I originally expected, I should do all right. So long as I get started by August, I can knock 500 over before the season closes.

Well, Mum, I will close now and will write to you every week until I get away.

With much love your affectionate son

11 JUNE 1936 — THURSDAY
Left the hospital — still very lame. Left Katherine on the train and went to Pine Creek.

12 JUNE 1936 — FRIDAY
Arrived Darwin 4.20 p.m. Train only about an hour late, which is a long way above average.

14 JUNE 1936 — SUNDAY
Left Darwin after dinner and went to Brocks Creek, 120 miles by road.

16 JUNE 1936 — TUESDAY
Left Pine Creek this morning with a big load of benzine and spares for the truck. Reached Arnhem Land Mine (84 miles). Put on a boy from the blacks' camp.

17 JUNE 1936 — WEDNESDAY
Left the mine this morning. Got a good early start but only went about 12 miles and hit a stump, breaking the stub axle. Sent the boy on to my camp at Kapalga with a letter

explaining matters and instructions to send a plant of horses back. Will probably take the boy three days to walk down and the horses two days to get back.

18 JUNE 1936 — THURSDAY
Sunk a soak in the creek bed for water. Got a good supply.

19 JUNE 1936 — FRIDAY
Went out hunting this morning for beef, only have about three days rations, got a kangaroo. Went out pigeon shooting after dinner. Returned to camp about 4 o'clock and found the boy taking life very easily. He calmly announced that he 'no more savvee that one country'. Fred and I decided to walk down to Kapalga.

20 JUNE 1936 — SATURDAY
Took our swags, consisting of blanket, mosquito net, a couple of days rations and the shotgun and started off for Kapalga. Went to Jim Jim Crossing for dinner. Had a couple of hours spell and went on after dinner. Tried to take a short cut through the swamps but couldn't get through — too much water. Shot a Burdekin duck. Camped in the swamps. My ankle's painful — very stiff and sore.

21 JUNE 1936 — SUNDAY
Woke up as stiff as a poker. Made Red Lily Crossing by dinner and battled on to the Leichhardt, then camped.

22 JUNE 1936 — MONDAY
Arrived at Kapalga just about dead beat. I reckon we walked over 20 miles, today, over rough plains and through long grass up to our waist. The grass is the worst to walk through. I hoped to find someone camped here but no luck. My ankle troubling me and Fred's old harpoon wound is troubling him. Only have a handful of flour left — made three Johnny cakes and found four ripe pawpaws, which was

our supper. Nothing on the lagoon to shoot, which is very unusual as Kapalga is noted for game. Finished flour.

23 JUNE 1936 — TUESDAY

Shot five bamboo pigeons — caught them coming in to water — made breakfast of them. After breakfast wrote a note and gave it to the boy with instructions to follow the freshest motor lorry tracks until he comes to my camp and deliver note. He should locate them by midday, expect them to be shooting down about Mongulla. If the motor lorry is there they ought to be back here today. Shot some squatter pigeons for dinner. Shot two Burdekin ducks. Nobody from camp.

24 JUNE 1936 — WEDNESDAY

Breakfasted off Burdekin duck that was shot yesterday. Later, we shot five Squatter Pigeons and as we were hungry we ate two of them, but saved three for dinner. Relief of Lucknow! — boy Clary arrived with packhorses and some food, which we wrapped ourselves around. After a feed we rode to buffalo camp, 15 miles on the West Alligator Plain.

26 JUNE 1936 — FRIDAY

Sam Mini brought his motor truck over from Wildman camp to cart hides into Kapalga Landing. *Maroubra* due 28th.

27 JUNE 1936 — SATURDAY

Loaded eighty odd hides. Left instructions for packhorse plant to come into Kapalga. Will go back to car from there and bring back three packloads of stuff we require. Went into Kapalga on Mini's truck. Police patrol just arrived — mounted Constables Littlejohn and Greville — all of us are very sorry to see them as they collected two guineas each off Sam Mini, Hazel Gaden and myself for aboriginal licences.

1 JULY 1936 — WEDNESDAY

Reached the car about midday. Packed everything I required into three sets of pack bags. Had a tough job balancing the

battery. Packed it well with grass. Took five drums of
benzine and planted them in three different places. Someone
might come along with ambitions to adopt some of it. Just as
I was ready to go Bert Coombs drove up in his truck with a
load of hides for Pine Creek. He and Ted Sawdy are
shooting the East Alligator. Both of us decided to camp and
have a yarn.

3 JULY 1936 — FRIDAY
Got to Kapalga about sundown and found everybody still
there. No boats arrived yet. *Maroubra* probably won't come
now as she is due round to Victoria River on the fourth.
Will try to ship a few hides on J. Gaden's boat the *Chantress*.
Feel very weak and washed out. Long way from being fit.
Won't be able to do any work this year.

4 JULY 1936 — SATURDAY
Boat for J. Gaden arrived early this morning — *Chantress*.
Was only able to ship 50 hides. Should have been a thousand
cartridges for me but they did not arrive. Had two tons of
salt on and a caddy (24 lb) of tobacco for me and five tons of
salt and stores for Hazel Gaden's camp. Got the cargo
unloaded and half the hides on by midnight.

5 JULY 1936 — SUNDAY
Got the *Chantress* away on this morning's tide. Went back to
the shooting camp. Will shift camp tomorrow.

9 JULY 1936 — THURSDAY
Camp out shooting. Returned early with seven hides.
McKercher and I caught horses and went for a tour of
inspection. Rode over to the Mongulla Range and climbed to
the top and had a good look round with my binoculars.
Could see Field Island and the sea, all low ranges to the
north. Does not appear to be suitable shooting country. Saw
plenty of buffalo on the plains. First time I have seen this
part of my country. Returned to camp well after dark.

Rather disappointed. Hoped to be able to get another camp
to the north but very unlikely.

10 JULY 1936 — FRIDAY
Camp out shooting. Self taking life easy.

13 JULY 1936 — MONDAY
Camp shooting. Self shot an old bull that strolled into the
camp. Shooters only came in with two hides so McKercher
and I went out and got a run on the plains and got another
five. I was riding horse called Nigger and got a fall that
shook me up a bit.

28 JULY 1936 — TUESDAY
Boat *Chantress* arrived after dinner. Went over to river to
meet Freddy Morris who returned with spare parts for his
car and my truck and a thousand cartridges. My truck has
cost me over £50 for spares and two tyres so far. Received
mail from Darwin agent and word from hide buyers. Hide
market still good. Boys found lost rifle.

31 JULY 1936 — FRIDAY
Hazel Gaden came over from his brother's camp to make
arrangements for his boys to go with him to shoot with Jack
Gaden. The latter has secured a sub-lease of 400 square miles
of Freer's country. Will leave me shorthanded. I will have to
go into Pine Creek (about 165 miles) as soon as I can fix the
truck up.

3 AUGUST 1936

Dear Mum

I wrote to you last month letting you know I had got out of
hospital and was heading back to the buffalo camp.
    When I left Katherine hospital I went down to Darwin
arriving on Friday June 12th. I went down to get a doctor to
have a look at me before I left as there was no resident doctor at

Katherine. The doctor said I could go, but at the same time didn't advise me to and cautioned me not to work or knock myself about. If I took it easy, he said I would get all right. I was very run down and weighed very little over nine stone.

Anyhow my friend Freddy Morris wanted to come out again and get a bit of shooting and take some more photos. We had arranged to go down in his car, a big Oldsmobile Six. It was a pretty tough proposition as there was about 150 miles of bush travelling, no roads at all and some sizeable swamps to circumnavigate.

We decided to follow the railway line to Pine Creek as it is a pretty good road, a distance of roughly 160 miles. We had decided to then leave the line at Pine Creek and go out through Arnhem Land Gold Mine, where there is a sort of a track in places, and down to Jim Jim Crossing and down the river (South Alligator) to Kapalga.

We left Darwin on Sunday after lunch and went to Brocks Creek (about 120 miles), which was a good run. Next day we went to Pine Creek. We took on 30 gallons of petrol there and left next morning. We camped at the mine that night, which was deserted except for a tribe of nomad blacks. This was a good day's run considering the nature of the country. We picked up a blackfellow there.

We got a flying start next morning as from the mine on there were no roads or tracks of any description, and so we anticipated a bit of work scrub cutting and perhaps making a creek crossing. We had high hopes of getting to a place called Ingarrabba that night, which is seven miles from Kapalga. Our hopes were dashed to the ground. We had gone about 20 or 30 miles and were cruising comfortably along at about 15 mph through a nice stretch of open country, when we hit a stump that was concealed by long grass. There was a crash and away the near side front wheel went spinning. We had broken a stub axle. It was a nice mess. We were well over 100 miles from the nearest town, and about 50 miles from Kapalga, and we had about a week's tucker at the outside with careful management.

We decided to send the blackfellow down to Kapalga with

a letter to Dave Cameron, instructing him to send back a packhorse plant and some tucker; so I wrote a letter and gave it to the blackfellow called Paddy and said 'You takem this letter, you findem my buffalo camp. Quick fella you go all the way. You no more sleep longa road.' I gave him some tucker and reckoned there was a fair chance of getting horses back in five or six days. We built a shed of boughs to provide shade and prepared to wait.

On the fourth day Paddy turned up and he still had the letter I gave him. 'I no more savvy that one country,' he explained.

There was only one thing to do now. We only had about a day's tucker left, so we packed it up, took the shotgun and a dozen cartridges and footed it. I'll never forget that stroll if I live for another hundred years. My ankle gave me hell. If there was a hole to walk into, I'd walk into it. If there was stump to hit, I'd hit it. The worst travelling was on the plains. The grass was waist high and it was rough sunbaked ground with big cracks in it. It took us three days to walk to Kapalga and after the first day we lived off the gun, shooting geese, ducks, pigeons and even curlew (which is very rank).

I expected Dave Cameron to be at Kapalga but the place was deserted. We were very disappointed as we were looking forward to a good square feed and had got quite enthusiastic during the last few miles. Dave had gone into Gaden's camp for company and I couldn't blame him. This is no country for a man to be on his own.

Fred and I were both just about settled. My ankle was like an oil drum and Fred was suffering from the effects of an accident he had, an alligator harpoon having gone through his stomach some years ago. We had all been on short rations. Both Fred and I would have been foolish to try and go any further. We certainly didn't have the ambition. We camped there the night and made our supper off some papaws that were growing wild round the lagoon.

The next morning I took Paddy and put him on the freshest tracks, which I told him to follow until he got to a camp. He did it all right this time and the next day a boy turned up with horses for us, and that same night we were down at the buffalo camp.

Gaden, who was running my camp under contract, had 300 down and a boat was due for a load of hides. So Fred decided to go into Darwin on her and get his stub axle and as I had decided to fit a new crown wheel in my truck, I reckoned it would be a good opportunity. Fred got both his part and mine up by plane and I don't know what Fred's cost him, but mine ran me into over £14 with freight.

Since all this, Fred has returned. Gaden has finished his contract (500) and gone and I have taken over my camp again. At the moment Fred is fitting the new crown wheel into my truck, which is over at Coorievar Spring (generally referred to as the Spring Camp) and should be back here by tomorrow. Then we are going up to his car to fit his stub axle, and then into Pine Creek for a load of tucker and pick up some more blacks somewhere, so I expect to get a go on shooting about the middle of this month. When Gaden was shooting for me he had his own team of blacks and now he has gone I am left with only one boy. As I am not properly right yet, I will have to try and get some experienced buffalo boys somewhere and just run the camp myself. I will have to be content with just paying my way this year.

This is about all there is to write about this time. As I am going to try and manage without going out shooting myself, I will have more time on my hands and try and write a little more oftener.

I intend shooting 450 hides before I knock off.

This letter should reach you somewhere around your birthday, so will wish you many happy returns of the day — this must be the first time I've thought of it.

Love to all at home, your loving son

4 AUGUST 1936 — TUESDAY
Went over to the landing this morning and branded 52 hides. Returned to camp and found Fred back with the truck.

Truck wants a good bit doing to her. Will probably do it in Pine Creek.

5 AUGUST 1936 — WEDNESDAY
Left this morning. Got within three miles of Kapalga and had trouble with the self starter. Fixed it up and went on. Had dinner on the Ingarrabba Plain. Just before sundown broke a steering arm. Got that riveted up by fire light.

6 AUGUST 1936 — THURSDAY
Went on again this morning. Got bogged in the wet sand in the Bamboo Crossing of the South Alligator River. Dug ourselves out and had dinner there. Went on and camped at Arnhem Land Gold Mine. We have a sort of a road on from here.

7 AUGUST 1936 — FRIDAY
Had a fair day's run. A spring clamp snapped but we fixed up a temporary job and reached Pine Creek easily. Missed the train down to Darwin. Usually goes Saturdays but went this morning this time.

8 AUGUST 1936 — SATURDAY
We fluked a car going to Darwin and Fred got a lift down. He can fix up all my business down there.

PINE CREEK

9 AUGUST 1936

Dear Mum

I arrived in Pine Creek with my truck and a load of hides the day before yesterday. I received a letter from you in my mail with a couple of quid in it for which many thanks. There is no date on your letter and the postmark is indistinct but it looks like April.

It is 163 miles by my speedometer from my camp to Pine

Creek, and it is mostly bush going with no roads and it is very rough.

I am very satisfied with the truck. It is a ton and a half and, although it has been knocked about a good deal, it has a great engine. We broke a steering arm coming in but didn't have much trouble fixing it; we riveted a piece of piping over the break.

I am sorry the photos were disappointing but hope to be able to send you some good ones later. Freddy Morris's photos have evidently gone astray. I think he made a mistake in the address. I suppose you know that every English £1 is worth £1 5s out here, the £20 was £25 when it arrived and the £2 was worth £2 10s.

I see you have a book on pearling. A friend of mine has a large pearling fleet in Darwin. I have been promising myself a trip 'down'. The fleet up here is pretty well all manned by Japanese diving, and Malay and Koepang deck hands. They have had a lot of bad luck these last two years, losing divers. Last year they lost seven. Six from diver's paralysis and one was bitten by a sea snake, which are death to anyone.

This year they have lost three from diver's paralysis, two disappeared, and one mauled by a shark. Buffalo shooting is a peaceable way of getting a living compared with that.

Love Tom

11 AUGUST 1936 — TUESDAY
Neville Hagearty flew Fred Morris back to Pine Creek in his Avro plane reaching here about 4.30.

12 AUGUST 1936 — WEDNESDAY
Gave Hagarty a hand to pull his engine down this morning. Went up with him for a test flight after dinner.

13 AUGUST 1936 — THURSDAY
Fred left by train for Katherine this morning to get some teeth pulled out (at least that's what he said). Fred came back from Katherine (minus three teeth) by railway section car with the manager of the N.T. Railways.

15 AUGUST 1936 — SATURDAY
Got away after dinner and went to Goodparla and camped.

16 AUGUST 1936 — SUNDAY
Went on this morning. Had dinner at the mine and picked
up boy called Ring. Camped at Fred's car. Fred put his stub
axle in.

17 AUGUST 1936 — MONDAY
Went on to Jim Jim. Left the truck there and Fred and I
went across on to the East Alligator to pick up blacks. Went
through sixty miles of pure bush, did in two tyres and one
tube. Didn't strike any blacks. Camped Barote Spring with
Bert Coombs who is carting hides across to the South
Alligator on the opposite side to where I am shooting.

22 AUGUST 1936 — SATURDAY
Decided to shift camp for a week and shoot where I saw the
buffalo yesterday. Shod the shooting horses and cut a big
hollow tree to make a water trough. Will sink a well at
Namundoot and camp there.

25 AUGUST 1936 — TUESDAY
Sent a boy out to get horses, Trinket and Adventure, but
only got Adventure. Trinket gone with the brumbies. Will
have to go out with a rifle tomorrow.

26 AUGUST 1936 — WEDNESDAY
Went out with a rifle to get Trinket. Cut across to Mongulla
to try and cut their tracks but couldn't strike them. Shot
three brumby stallions.

27 AUGUST 1936 — THURSDAY
Riding all the morning. Cut Trinket's tracks late this
afternoon. Boy went after her and brought her back. Shot
three more brumbies.

28 AUGUST 1936 — FRIDAY
Went out shooting and one man got lost and disorganised the
day's shooting. Sent all the boys out on his tracks and
tracked him into the camp!

5 SEPTEMBER 1936 — SATURDAY
Returned to camp and found Paul Bynum from the other
side of the river had come across with word Bert Coombs
died of thirst last week.

7 SEPTEMBER 1936 — MONDAY
Fred took the truck back to Mongulla to finish carting the
hides. He will build a jetty and bark house at the landing to
stack the hides in until the next trip of the *Maroubra*.

13 SEPTEMBER 1936 — SUNDAY
Poor day, two boys and myself got a touch of fever.

14 SEPTEMBER 1936 — MONDAY
Camp sick no shooting.

18 SEPTEMBER 1936 — FRIDAY
Clary and myself out shooting. Two kids driving the pack
horses. Not enough water in the well here to give the horses
a good drink so put in until midnight deepening it and
watering the horses.

21 SEPTEMBER 1936 — MONDAY
Two boys still sick. Clary and self out shooting with the two
kids driving the packhorses. They generally get lost in the
scrub two or three times a day and we have to track them
up. Clary's horse galloped into a tree with him today, hurt
him and smashed the saddle.

23 SEPTEMBER 1936 — WEDNESDAY
Very sick — a touch of malaria.

24 SEPTEMBER 1936 — THURSDAY
Still feel very sick, rundown and out of order.

26 SEPTEMBER 1936 — SATURDAY
Fred Morris returned from his trip to Darwin — only eleven
days overdue — he'd hit a few trees and bent his car up a
bit.

30 SEPTEMBER 1936 — WEDNESDAY
Carted hides into Kapalga and met the *Maroubra* — received
two tons of salt and some fencing wire and general cargo —
shipped 206 hides. Loaded salt onto the truck and returned to
camp.

ALLIGATOR RIVER

5 OCTOBER 1936

Dear Mum

Received your letter the other day by the *Maroubra* when she
came round for a load of hides. It was dated August 18th and
written on the beach.

I am pretty right now and have been shooting since August.
I expect to shoot right into November if the storms hold off,
that is, until the 15th. This is of course pretty late, but I'll have
to raise the average somehow.

We are having a terrible year for water here. There isn't a
drop of water on my Kapalga lease, although there is plenty on
the Wildman side but it is pretty well shot out.

A buffalo shooter (Bert Coombs) got bushed and died of
thirst on the other side of the South Alligator River, not long
ago. The Alligator down here is all salt water. Fred Morris and
I were the last white men to see him alive. I went over to see
him to arrange for him to send his hides into Darwin by the
Maroubra — I wanted to get 400 or 500 hides for her to make the
trip profitable and I only anticipated having 200 or 300 hides
myself. He agreed to do this and asked my advice regarding a

suitable place to make a landing. I advised him to use a place known to the natives as Min-mi-larri. They started off with a load of hides in an old utility truck pulled by horses he had taken the engine out of. He got it into his head that Min-mi-larri was up the river from my landing, whereas it was lower. He had an argument with his 'boy' (Bamboo Charlie) and left him and he got properly bushed and perished a few days later.

My truck is going all right. I have got 270 hides since the contractors finished shooting. With their lot, it makes a total of 770 shot here so far. I hope to get another 300. So by the time I knock off these ridges will have had a good trimming up. Hides are still a good price and there are a lot of shooters out. I don't think there is a buffalo on the coast that hasn't been chased or shot at this year, and they're getting damned hard to find.

I'm still a few quid behind it. I've paid off over £400 and will square up easily enough, but it's pretty hard when a fellow knows that he should have made close on £1000. If things had gone all right, I would have started shooting early in May as it was I never fired a shot until 20th August. However, I ought to do all right next year. (It's always next year.)

Will try and write you later.

Love to all

7 OCTOBER 1936 — WEDNESDAY
Will have to go to Darwin tomorrow on urgent business.

8 OCTOBER 1936 — THURSDAY
We started this morning with the truck and car — shot seven bulls and sent them back to the camp in the truck — went on by car. Got to Adelaide River and camped. A good day's run — over 100 miles.

9 OCTOBER 1936 — FRIDAY
Arrived Darwin about 2.30 p.m.

15 OCTOBER 1936 — THURSDAY
Left Darwin this morning. Put a boy on from the blacks'
camp, three miles out of town. Went to Rum Jungle and hit a
rock, smashing the engine bolts and front engine plate. Wired
it down and went on. Got to Adelaide River and camped.

16 OCTOBER 1936 — FRIDAY
Ran into the Margaret River and smashed a back spring.
Fixed it up and went on and camped at Moon Billabong on
the Mary River.

17 OCTOBER 1936 — SATURDAY
Went on to shooting camp.

18 OCTOBER 1936 — SUNDAY
Ran over to Moon Camp in the truck and picked up Jack
Knight, one boy and his lubra, 16 dogs and a pig.

26 OCTOBER 1936 — MONDAY
Charlie Payne turned up from up the river to borrow salt.
Bought a hundred head of heifers off him to be delivered
about the end of November.

30 OCTOBER 1936 — FRIDAY
Good storm last night. Buffalo split and scattered. Hell west
and crooked.

1 NOVEMBER 1936 — SUNDAY
Shifted camp to Gypsy Spring. Well water putrid. Deepened
and cleaned well. Built bark house.

2 NOVEMBER 1936 — MONDAY
Got twenty-one hides today. Good day's shooting. Very
short of water here. If we get a good day's shooting
tomorrow will shift the next day and knock off shooting for
the season. With Gaden's contract over a thousand hides shot
here this season.

8 November 1936 — Sunday
Went up to Ingarrabba where I will build a station. Lagoon
nearly dry. Sent a boy with the horses to camp at the
Leichhardt until it rains (six miles away).

9 November 1936 — Monday
Jack Knight sinking a well. I'm cutting and carting timber
for buildings and yards. Jack got down seven feet. One boy
and self cut and carted 70 rails. Will need about 400 rails and
100 posts for stockyard. A lot of work to be done.

10 November 1936 — Tuesday
Jack Knight got water at 12 feet. Cut and carted 80 rails.
One boy stripping bark.

11 November 1936 — Wednesday
Getting big timber to build a wagon shed. Will put up a
building large enough to house everything for a start and
build a homestead later. Cut a trough out of a hollow log.
This lagoon never been so dry before.

16 November 1936 — Monday
Rode to Kapalga.

17 November 1936 — Tuesday
Maroubra tied up at 8.30 a.m. Unloaded ½ ton of flour, 1 ton
of general cargo and 2 tons of salt. Loaded 327 hides and
sailed 9 p.m. Started to get my loading across the plain,
which is boggy from recent rains and on to the ridges, about
a mile away.

18 November 1936 — Wednesday
I got everything to Ingarrabba and saw Gaden. Jack Knight
bought the *Chantress* off him. He will have to go into town
in a few days to take delivery of it. He has decided to lay
her up in the river here and stay with me for the wet.

INGARRABBA STATION
ALLIGATOR RIVER
NORTH AUSTRALIA

19 NOVEMBER 1936

Dear Mum

I s'pose it's about time you heard from me.

I have finished shooting for the season and have got 1060 hides, counting 500 that Gaden shot for me under contract and, although I had to scratch to get them, I am well satisfied. It has been a disastrous year in one way as had it not been for my accident I would have cleared £1000. However, had hides not been the price they were, I wouldn't have pulled through. As it is, I am just about on my feet.

When I left the hospital in June I owed a little over £600, but I have pretty well got squared up, renewed a couple of promissory notes, which I can pretty well cover, and have bought 100 head of cows for breeders and am forming a cattle station here. I have selected a lagoon on the South Alligator River, called Ingarrabba by the natives, and I'm calling my station after it. I am starting to build and have a big shed built of bush timber and bark roof, which will easily withstand several wet seasons. The rainfall is a little over 60 inches.

Then, I have fencing wire and will put up about a mile of fencing to start with for a horse paddock. I have half the timber cut to build a big stockyard, in which I will be able to work 500 head of cattle, draft, brand, and break in horses. This yard will take over 500 rails, 12 feet long and 5 inches across, at the small end, and 150 posts. It will take two years to complete as I will only be able to work on it during the off season. My motor lorry, which has been running well all the year, has been a wonderful help carting timber, etc.

My leg is pretty good now and no one could tell I have anything wrong with it while I have my boot on. Of course it is naturally weaker than the other foot, but I can walk all right, but can't run. Anyhow, I'm always on a horse so it doesn't matter much. I have really only been back to my old form for about a month; it is only since then that I have been able to stand up to a decent day's work. Previously, I had to keep having a day or so off now and then during the shooting, and have been employing men. Not very satisfactory either. It's hard to get men to stand up to this work, more especially in my camp. In fact it's a saying on the coast here 'If you want to do six months hard work go into Tom Cole's camp for a month'. Anyhow, I pay higher rates than anybody else to black and white alike. Not because I like parting with the money, but because I've got to, to keep them. Anyhow they earn it.

I have just got over a frenzied couple of days. The *Maroubra* has just been and unloaded my wet season supplies. It took my last consignment of hides away, about 320, and I have been getting my cargo up to the station on the lorry. We copped a good storm and had the devil's own job getting across a plain about a mile wide. I was afraid we were going to get some more rain as the first storms are just beginning to fall and it's dangerous being far out with a motor lorry now. Anyhow, everything is in now and I can hop into a bit of solid work for about six weeks. Then, the big rains are well set in and I shall have to keep indoors for the next month or so and can do up my harness, gear and plant and overhaul my truck.

I was in Darwin early in October and Lord Semphill's Monospar aeroplane was the latest sensation there. I know all the aerodrome fellows and always look up the Qantas Empire Airways crowd when in town.

Bunting was Director of Civil Aviation then. Since then he's been promoted and a great friend of mine has the position, and he was hitting the roof about the Monospar crowd blaming the Darwin bearing for the Monospar going astray. Hagearty, who is the Qantas Manager here, told me that it was childish. The Darwin directional wireless has been bringing in two planes a week across the Timor Sea for ages, and its accuracy has never been questioned. All the Qantas pilots have complete faith in it. Anyhow, the Darwin crowd have, I believe, forced an inquiry.

Hagearty has his own plane and he took me up for a flight.

It was the first time I had been up and I enjoyed the experience. I would like to own a plane. They would be just the thing out here, isolated like I am. During the wet season I'm practically marooned out here and apart from an aeroplane, which is a long way ahead, the only means of communication is by boat.

I am pretty lucky, however. I intended buying a launch but a chap I have had working for me has bought the lugger *Chantress* — a well known boat that has been running around the coast here. In 1934 she took my hides from the Wildman River.

The chap that has bought her, Jack Knight, wanted to lay her up for the wet in the river here. I was only too glad of the opportunity to have a boat available and so I gave him the freedom of my place for the wet. It suits him well enough as it won't cost him anything to live.

There will be three white men here now as I still have Dave Cameron with me. I have had him since '33 and I don't think he'll ever leave me. He is a great old fellow and does the cooking and looks after the camp and so on. When I'm away I can leave him in charge and I know everything is right. This is a big consideration out here as at times we see large numbers of natives walking about. A fellow couldn't leave a camp with any rations in it when they are around. I get a supply to do me for six months at a time, so I've got to look after it. I never order less than half a ton of flour and always get a quarter of a ton of sugar, and everything else I get in bulk. I am sometimes feeding 20 natives alone. If a crowd of Myall (bush blacks) natives got into my ration supply, they could have a great play-about.

Packhorses are going into Darwin, or rather I should say, into the telegraph line, starting tomorrow. Jack Knight is going into Darwin to take the *Chantress* over. He will ride as far as Bachelor Siding and will catch the weekly train there. He leaves here Monday and should get to the line on Saturday. He should be back into the river with the lugger in about a fortnight. He will then take a load of hides in for Gaden, so I will be able to write you again.

Now that I have settled down and have a permanent

address. I am going to get you to send me a couple of Xmas puddings at Christmas time. You may be able to get them to me quicker by sending them Singapore way, which is a lot shorter, I know. In fact, I think that would be the best way to send all the mail. I would enquire if I were you.

By the way, did I tell you I have (as far as is known) a Northern Territory record. I sent a bull hide in from here, going 170 pounds dry weight! This a colossal hide. A 'big' bullock hide is around 50 pounds dry weight. I also sent 33 hides to Brisbane and they realized £75 16s. They were shot in four days. Cannot think of any more news.

Love to all and best wishes for a very happy Xmas and the best of New Years.

Love Tom

20 NOVEMBER 1936 — FRIDAY
Took a couple of pack horses and a boy and went for a ride up the river for a look around. Camped Malara. Some bush blacks here, none of whom could speak English. Some very good grazing country up here. Very few buffalo judging by the tracks and only saw one old bull on his own. Saw the tracks of two horses watering at Geena.

23 NOVEMBER 1936 — MONDAY
Built a fowl house and put some more time in on the shed. Have it nearly completed now. Got the roof finished, it took four lorry loads of bark.

24 NOVEMBER 1936 — TUESDAY
Working around the place all the morning, built a fireplace and did a few odd jobs. Young cyclone blew up this evening, got an inch of badly needed rain out of it and the blacks had their humpies blown away.

25 NOVEMBER 1936 — WEDNESDAY
Blacks had to rebuild their humpies and I put some finishing touches to my domicile. Dave made a batch of bread from

new yeast today and it was prime — the best he's turned out
this year. Evidently the hops have been at fault all the time
and he'd been blaming the water and flour alternately. Boy
turned up with letter from Payne stating he is leaving to
muster my 100 head of breeders, immediately.

28 NOVEMBER 1936 — SATURDAY

Cut and carted all the stockyard posts and found I had made
a miscalculation with the length. They should have been
seven foot six inches long and I made the measuring sticks
seven foot. Will have to throw a lot out and cut some more.
All good ironwood timber too. Anyhow it will do for the
paddock fence. The big posts for gateways are 13′ 6″
ironwood and 1′ at the small end and it was as much as four
strong boys and myself could do to get them on the truck.
We spent half an hour juggling one with skids and levers.

3 DECEMBER 1936 — THURSDAY

Ring came up this morning and said he wanted to go for a
'walkabout', so had to let him go. Big corroboree over on
the East Alligator River and the blacks here are very
restless. I will have my work cut out holding the working
boys for the next week. If they made up their minds to go I
will have to let them go or they will only leave anyway. Cut
and carted rails today. Big storm worked up this afternoon
but proved dry and we only got a few spits and a lot of
wind.

4 DECEMBER 1936 — FRIDAY

Clary and Diamond returned. Brought word that the
Chantress hit a reef off Gun Point, and the skipper dumped
220 hides of Gaden's and beached her. Jack Knight went into
see if anything can be done to her. Gaden had written to me
but the boys lost the letter and made up the loss by giving
me an old bill they found at an old camp.

9 DECEMBER 1936 — WEDNESDAY
Sent a couple of boys out for beef this morning. A boy from
Gaden's over with a note from Hazel — *Maroubra* due
tomorrow — will have to go to Kapalga in the morning.

12 DECEMBER 1936 — SATURDAY
No boat. Three good days wasted. Gaden mustered horses.
Trinket, the crack shooting mare, turned up in the muster.

17 DECEMBER 1936 — THURSDAY
Got things together for the trip in. Oiled the packs, riding
saddles and all the hobbles and gear. Got a fortnight's supply
of rations. Should get an early start tomorrow morning.
Will take two boys (Diamond and Clary), two packs, two
packhorses and two saddle horses each.

18 DECEMBER 1936 — FRIDAY
Got away this morning and had to ride all day before we
could get a drink of water. When we struck water and
camped, it poured with rain!

20 DECEMBER 1936 — SUNDAY
Reached Goodparla Station.

21 DECEMBER 1936 — MONDAY
Mustering camp — mustering my breeders here. Making
very poor progress only about 40 in hand. Arranged to stop
mustering owing to unsuitable weather. Too hot and cattle
getting knocked about too much. Will take delivery after
the wet. Gave them a hand to brand a few calves.

25 DECEMBER 1936 — FRIDAY
Pine Creek

PINE CREEK
NORTHERN TERRITORY

25 DECEMBER 1936

Dear Mum

I have just come into Pine Creek from the station and expect to
be in for some time, that is, for the wet season, anyhow.

I think I told you that I had bought a mob of cattle and they
were being mustered off Goodparla, an adjoining station, and
were to be delivered in November. I built a stockyard in
readiness for them, but they didn't arrive. So I decided by the
middle of December to ride in and see what they were doing.
Goodparla Station is my closest neighbour and is owned by the
Stevens Brothers. Fred Stevens runs the place. I can go by horse
in two days; it is about fifty miles away.

When I got there they were mustering my heifers but only
had 35 in hand. Fred Stevens had to go to Darwin practically
straight away and would be away a fortnight, which meant
that the mustering would not be resumed until the middle of
January. By then, the wet season would have set in, and the
chances of getting them through would have been very poor —
they would have had to be watched at night — and cattle are
the very devil at night in the rain. This wouldn't have affected
me greatly as I was only paying for what was delivered, but I
wouldn't get a mob of cattle as cheap as that again and I wanted
them.

The man I bought them off got them in lieu of wages, and
he was the one who was going to lose with every beast he lost,
and his horses weren't half good enough to hold them. So the
upshot of it was, I called the muster off and gave him a cheque
for £40 for the lot, which is a tenner lower than the original
price, but I have to take delivery of them myself at Goodparla.

Since then I have bought another 100 off a very old friend of
mine, Dick Guild. I have given a lot more for them, but they
will be worth it to me as there will be male cattle in them,
which will be saleable in a few years. Dick will deliver them to
Ingarrabba for me and will also pick up the other 100 at

Goodparla on the way down and bring them also, so we are killing two stones with one bird as it were.

I have taken a job for a couple of months. I am slaughtering bullocks, which will bring in a few quid during the wet season. With luck, I may be able to start shooting again with a square start. Until then, I will be in touch with Darwin as I am only 20 miles out at the slaughter yard. Cars run in and out all the time, so I will be getting my mail as often as I want it.

I spent a quiet Xmas with the Stevens. They are station owners and butchers around Pine Creek, and the two sons own Goodparla. I am returning to Ingarrabba Station about March and hope to be shooting by May. I hope you all spent an enjoyable Xmas and hope you have an enjoyable New Year. Will send you some photos that I took of the start of Ingarrabba Station.

Love to all

1937

DARWIN
NORTHERN TERRITORY

23 JANUARY 1937

Dear Mum

I just received your last letter and the newspaper cutting.

I am staying out at Koolpinyah Station, 30 miles from Darwin. The Herbert brothers own it. Evan Herbert is a great friend of mine. They have just started a butchering venture and I am giving them a bit of assistance for a couple of months. Then I will return to my place. They have a very nice property carrying about 5000 head of cattle, but like all cattle men here have been through a pretty thin time and started butchering to get an outlet for their cattle. Their father used to be chief justice here and later government resident. He then went to Papua as chief justice and was acting administrator. He went from there to Norfolk Island as administrator, where he died.

I am writing this from Darwin as we are in for the weekend. I must close now to catch the mail.

Love to all

P.S. I have bought another mob of cattle, which is to be delivered next year (100 head of mixed sex and age). I now have 200 altogether.

DARWIN
NORTHERN TERRITORY

24 MARCH 1937

Dear Mum

I am writing this letter aboard the *Maroubra*, which is loaded
with my stores and salt, and I am headed back for the Alligator
to start shooting. The engines are vibrating terribly and it
makes me write all crinkly. We are running against the tide
with a heavy sea and will get into the mouth of the river
tonight. The skipper will anchor there as he doesn't like
running round this coast at night as it isn't charted and is pretty
dirty. We get to Kapalga tomorrow and will unload my stuff
there. I have eight tons on.

We are three days out of Darwin and dropped the light-
house mails last night. Tomorrow we head for Kapalga landing. (Thirty miles up the river.)

We had a cyclone in Darwin a couple of weeks before I left,
which wrecked the place properly.

We got word through the meteorologist stationed at the
aerodrome that there was one in the vicinity of Bathurst Island
heading for the west coast, but it took a twist and started to
blow about 9 o'clock. I was in a cafe with a couple of friends,
who were celebrating striking it rich in the goldfields and had
come into Darwin on the last plane. The next thing we knew
the power house failed and all the lights went out. The wind
was hitting at about 70 miles an hour then.

Another friend of mine, who is a newspaper reporter and
lives near where I stay, was to drive me home. But when we
went to where his car was parked, the headlights were smashed
by a fallen tree and the hood had been ripped off (and hasn't
been seen since). The next thing was to get a car home but cars
were at a premium that night. Eventually, I got a taxi home
(two and a half miles from town) and very glad I was to get
there as Mrs Morris was on her own. My friend Fred was away
in Sydney on leave and Mr Morris was over at the aerodrome
standing by the mail planes. He works there.

The wind registered a speed of 100 miles an hour and it was pretty hair-raising. Darwin depends for its water supply on wells and all houses have wells, and most had windmills, B.C. — Before Cyclone. Our windmill, water supply tank and tank stand went early in the night. They were blown over and the concrete foundations were torn up, and a lot of big trees were uprooted around the house. Also, a couple of sheets of iron were lifted off the roof, but that was all the damage. When the iron went off, I expected the roof to roll up like a carpet, but it stuck to it well.

The scenes of chaos and desolation in the morning were indescribable. The buildings here are all constructed for tropical conditions and a lot are up on piles or stumps, which vary in height from 1 to 7 feet. The houses were just rolled off their stumps and turned inside out, roofs were blown off galore, and there wasn't more than two windmills left in the whole of Darwin. Telephone poles were blown over and the wireless station was out of action. The Overland Telegraph Line was down and Darwin had no communication with the outside world for 48 hours. The wireless station was the first to establish contact with an emergency set.

They tell me it was only a small cyclone, but I never was greedy where cyclones were concerned.

The astonishing part of the whole business was that there was only one death, although there were a few injured.

Well I'm afraid I can't write you any more as this is going by aerial mail and as there isn't any more news of interest to you, I will close.

With love to everybody, your loving son

25 MARCH 1937 — THURSDAY
Reached Kapalga landing on *Maroubra*. Unloaded my loading (8 tons) and the *Maroubra* left on the same tide. I had to walk up to the station — arrived 1 a.m. — everything okay, just out of tucker.

27 MARCH 1937 — SATURDAY
Started to pull the truck down.

28 MARCH 1937 — SUNDAY
Started work on the bearings. Had a job with the sump.
Straightened steering arm. Boy mustered all the horses. All
here, good condition, ready for work.

29 MARCH 1937 — MONDAY
Worked on the truck all the morning. Put new oil in and
greased it. Started work on the pack saddles after dinner.
Will have to make 2 sets of pack bags and a pack saddle also
need to repair 5 pack saddles.

30 MARCH 1937 — TUESDAY
Cut out leather for two sets of bags and one pack saddle.
Lots of tedious and heavy sewing to be done. Twenty-four
feet of double sewing in a set of pack bags.

8 APRIL 1937 — THURSDAY
Started on the truck again after dinner. Can't get it to start.
Something wrong with the ignition. I don't know one end of
it from the other.

9 APRIL 1937 — FRIDAY
Got the truck running for a while this morning then it
stopped with a bang.

10 APRIL 1937 — SATURDAY
Started unscrewing things to get the gear box out and
decided I'd have to take the engine out. Got the engine half
out and found I *could* get the gear box out. Finally got it out
but none the wiser. Heaven alone knows if I'll ever get it
together again.

11 APRIL 1937 — SUNDAY
Motor lorry from one end of Ingarrabba to the other.

Examined clutch, front gear box and back gear box. Can't
see anything wrong. Started to assemble it.

12 APRIL 1937 — MONDAY
Worked on the truck all the morning. Found a place for
almost everything. Eventually got it stuck together. Will
probably have to get spares up by plane. I can see a lot of
expense ahead of me but will have to get it going somehow.

16 APRIL 1937 — FRIDAY
Mick Madigan, a buffalo shooter from the other side, turned
up here this morning. Looking for his partner, Paul Bynum.
Mick has been away from his camp some time and when he
returned he found it deserted. Believes something may have
happened to him. I have heard nothing of him. Decided to
report the matter.

17 APRIL 1937 — SATURDAY
Decided to ride to Arnhem Land Mine and send a letter in to
police reporting Bynum missing. Madigan and I rode
together as far as the river crossing about 25 miles and split
there. Advised him to continue searching through the Jim
Jim swamps.

18 APRIL 1937 — SUNDAY
Reached the mine after a hard day's ride. Roberts leaving for
Pine Creek next Wednesday.

19 APRIL 1937 — MONDAY
Paul Bynum arrived here just before midnight last night
riding a horse that was all in. He had met Madigan at Jim
Jim Crossing and rode up to the mine to stop the letter going
in. Packed up and made back. Rode through some very nice
stock country which is still crown lands. Would like to take
it up.

20 APRIL 1937 — TUESDAY
Got a late start. Didn't wake until clear daylight and never
got off until sunrise. Got home about 3 o'clock. Camp
getting up to working strength. Boys are here now.

29 APRIL 1937 — THURSDAY
Had a bit of trouble on my way back to camp. Got stuck in a
creek for a start and had to unload the salt and carry it
across. Later the fan broke in half and nearly went through
the radiator. Later lost the fan belt. Suppose it broke.

30 APRIL 1937 — FRIDAY
Had to cut a mud guard up to make a fan, only suitable
material. Put a new tyre on the front before I get a blow
out. Will have to get out shooting and stir things up a bit.

12 MAY 1937 — WEDNESDAY
Loaded the truck with hides and started for Kapalga landing.
Got two miles and the casting broke at the water pump
where it is bolted on to the engine block. Fan broke again.
Maroubra left on this morning's tide. Things a bit messed up
now.

25 MAY 1937 — TUESDAY
To Darwin on the special. Sent my horses back to Marrakia
Station with boy. Will come out from Darwin by car to
Marrakia.

31 MAY 1937 — MONDAY
Left Darwin with Lou Curnock by car this morning.
Intended to go through to Marrakia but Adelaide River is
uncrossable with car, so crossed by canoe and walked to
Marrakia arriving at about midnight.

1 JUNE 1937 — TUESDAY
Sent packs back to the river this morning for the gear I
brought from Darwin.

5 June 1937 — Saturday

Got to the Four Mile camp early and got the truck running, but not so good as it boils too quickly. I will have to make a few adjustments tomorrow.

14 June 1937 — Monday

Went back to the camp this morning for the last load of hides. Started to build a jetty. Boat due today or tomorrow. I wonder how many days late she'll be this time? Food supplies are very low in the camp.

C/- Cousin & Co
Darwin

14 June 1937

Dear Mum

Just a hurried note that I am writing under my truck on the bank of the river at my Mongulla landing, where I'm waiting for the *Maroubra*. I am shipping away my first load of hides for this season, about 170.

I started shooting April 26th and did very badly for a while; I couldn't seem to drop on to them. Am getting a few more now, however, and I think I can knock over a steady 200 per month till October.

I am enclosing a few newspaper cuttings that I thought may interest you. The southern press seems to have got hold of me, I have certainly been in the news. I understand I have been broadcasted over the wireless — a lot of tripe about interesting and romantic personality of Northern Territory... cool headed, crack shot, superb horseman, in among a tribe of natives known to be hostile... and so on and so on — all rot of course. The bit about me being marooned is sheer imagination, there is no foundation for it whatever.

These cuttings come to the government offices. The Northern Territory administration subscribe to a press cutting agency and anything connected with the Territory is sent up.

Freddy Morris pinches anything interesting. I had several
more; I appear to have displaced Mrs Simpson as a news item. I
expect it will all die down.

Hope you are all in good health. How are the boys doing?

Give my love to everybody, your affectionate son
P.S. I have an old camera, I swapped a rifle for it. I don't know
if it works yet, but am trying it and may be able to send you a
few snaps later.

15 JUNE 1937 — TUESDAY
Finished jetty. No boat.

16 JUNE 1937 — WEDNESDAY
Mission launch went up the river this morning. They advise
that *Maroubra* loaded on the 15th but may wait and take the
Millimgimbi loading out, which means she won't be here
until the 25th. We will be right out of rations long before
that.

26 JUNE 1937 — SATURDAY
Waiting for word from the landing that *Maroubra* arrived.
There are no rations left in the camp and, what is worse, no
tobacco. Natives very unsettled — will have a job to keep
the camp going.

28 JUNE 1937 — MONDAY
Situation getting serious. Will take a load of hides into Pine
Creek with the truck and bring a load of rations back. Can
only drive in the daytime, no lights.

30 JUNE 1937 — WEDNESDAY
Got away at the first crack of dawn. Hit an ant hill about
midday and smashed the clutch housing. Wired it up and
went on. Drove for 14 hours today without stopping and
only covered 66 miles.

2 JULY 1937 — FRIDAY
To Pine Creek. Sold hides for a good price. Wired to
Sydney for a new clutch housing. No word from Darwin
regarding *Maroubra* whereabouts. Hides dropping in price.
Secured contract to supply 500 at 6¾ pence.

3 JULY 1937 — SATURDAY
Messing about nearly all day getting things finalised. Loaded
up with rations and benzine and got away just before
sundown. Headlights didn't work too well.

5 JULY 1937 — MONDAY
Got back to the camp at dark. Speedometer registered over
400 miles. Boat had arrived on the 30th, so have a good
supply of rations now.

6 JULY 1937 — TUESDAY
Gave the camp a day off. Self to Kapalga with Mick
Madigan and a native canoe. *Maroubra* has left his cargo on
the wrong side of the river, so he will have to cross it over.

12 JULY 1937 — MONDAY
Clary came down from station with letter from Guild —
will have to go up tomorrow and take delivery of 280 head
of cattle, 20 horses and two mules.

13 JULY 1937 — TUESDAY
Took delivery of cattle and inspected them. Bought eighteen
horses and two mules from Dick Guild.

14 JULY 1937 — WEDNESDAY
Put the cattle out on the plains and sent twelve head of fresh
horses down to the camps.

16 JULY 1937 — FRIDAY
Left the station this morning. Steering locked on the left
lock, hit a tree and smashed the headlights and brackets off.

The crack in the chassis opened up a bit more and the axle badly bent.

21 JULY 1937 — WEDNESDAY
Shooting up the West Alligator River. Mare shied off from a charging bull and galloped into a tree — with me — got shook up a bit.

24 JULY 1937 — SATURDAY
Had a look at the cattle, seem to have settled down all right.

30 JULY 1937 — FRIDAY
Made plans for a big day's shooting which didn't work out. Got into some jungle that a dog couldn't bark in. Saw a good few bulls but couldn't seem to hit them.

3 AUGUST 1937 — TUESDAY
I'm having trouble with the carburettor owing to a lubra filling the petrol tank with water instead of filling the radiator. She used a tea billy and I can't get the tea leaves out.

4 AUGUST 1937 — WEDNESDAY
Got all the hides to the landing and will stack and brand the rest of them tomorrow. Boat may come and may not — probably not. Will have to get into Darwin pretty soon.

8 AUGUST 1937 — SUNDAY
Got away this morning, but got bogged on the plains, then got stuck in the sand, and just before sundown the radiator burst.

8 AUGUST 1937 — MONDAY
Camped at the Lakes last night. Fixed up the radiator this morning — only went three miles and got condenser trouble. Pushed on and camped on the Mary River. Bad crossing here — will have to corduroy to get across.

10 AUGUST 1937 — TUESDAY

Corduroyed the crossing and crossed the river this morning.
Had to pull up and build up the chassis, where it is broken.
Went on and camped at Marrakia.

11 AUGUST 1937 — WEDNESDAY

Left Marrakia and went on. Generator broke about two
miles from Marrakia. Went on. Ran out of benzine at the 22
mile. Borrowed a drum and went on to Darwin.

12 AUGUST 1937 — THURSDAY

Put the truck into a garage for overhaul. Will have to wait
for next Thursday's plane for spares.

25 AUGUST 1937 — WEDNESDAY

Left Darwin and camped at Humpty Doo Station.

26 AUGUST 1937 — THURSDAY

Lost my crank handle somewhere between Marrakia and the
Mary River.

27 AUGUST 1937 — FRIDAY

Reached the camp at the Stony Point — 78 hides shot here.
Been held up waiting for me to return with cartridges.

30 AUGUST 1937 — MONDAY

Went back to landing with last load of hides. *Maroubra*
arrived on time for once in her career. Couldn't tie up to the
jetty till midnight.

1 SEPTEMBER 1937 — WEDNESDAY

To the station with Dave and to do a job or two. Body to be
put on the truck, crank handle to be made, cattle and horses
to be looked at. Visit from Harry Stott, who is shooting up
the river.

17 SEPTEMBER 1937 — FRIDAY
Got an early start this morning and went 50 miles and a
piston broke. Lucky enough to get horses off a man camped
close to here catching dingoes. Will ride down to the camp
and get fresh horses and return to Darwin and buy another
truck. Went about ten miles in the moonlight.

24 SEPTEMBER 1937 — FRIDAY
Reached Darwin about eleven a.m.

25 SEPTEMBER 1937 — SATURDAY
Bought a Ford V8 40 cwt truck, which had come up on the
last boat and is practically new.

3 OCTOBER 1937 — SUNDAY
Maroubra arrived — unloaded flour, roofing iron, fencing
wire, coarse salt and general cargo.

7 OCTOBER 1937 — THURSDAY
Started to put piston on old truck and broke a ring.

8 OCTOBER 1937 — FRIDAY
Made another start on the truck this morning. Broke another
ring and decided to tow it. Broke the chain twice in 100
yards, so pulled her down again and put the piston in and ran
her back to the station. I got back in the dark.

9 OCTOBER 1937 — SATURDAY
Pushed the old truck into a shed this morning — made the
sign of the cross and left her. I went back to the buffalo
camp.

20 OCTOBER 1937 — WEDNESDAY
To Kapalga with a load of hides and then up to the station
with half a ton of barbed wire. Harry Stott is here to repair
saddles and gear.

23 October 1937 — Saturday

Built a bark house and a horseyard. Harry Stott started saddling.

25 October 1937 — Monday

To the Stony Point camp for some bees wax for the saddler.

Kapalga
Alligator River

3 November 1937

Dear Mum

Just a short note in a hurry. Today is the last day's shooting for the season. Both my camps are knocking off today. They have not come back in with today's hides yet, so I don't know what the exact tally will be, but anyhow it is over 1400.

I got 400 hides for October, which was my best month, July was the next best, 300. I haven't had any returns since August but I expect the total to be well over £2000. Of course, my overhead has been correspondingly increased — I have three men on high wages and I bought a mob of cattle and a new V8 truck — however, I am ahead of it at last, and what a struggle. Looking back it seems worse than it did at the time. I wouldn't like to go through it again.

I am considering buying a business — station and butchery. Preliminary negotiations are in progress. It has been under offer to me for some time and is cheap. I am going in to inspect it at about the end of the month. If I decide to take it I shall put a manager in there, and I have a good man in view. It will be a lot better for me as I will be closer to civilization. The butchery is killing five to seven bullocks a week, besides pigs and goats (which take the place of sheep out here). The station that goes with it has 1000 and 1500 head of cattle on it, a piggery, numerous buildings, a car and truck, refrigerating plant, etc., and — what appeals to me — a steady income. This buffalo shooting fluctuates terribly, one year they are a good price, next you can't give them away.

I will write to you later and let you know how things are going. Must close now. The *Maroubra* is due on the 6th but there's no telling when she'll be here.

Love to everybody, your loving son

7 NOVEMBER 1937 — SUNDAY
Maroubra tied up 9 a.m. — unloaded cargo and loaded half the hides.

8 NOVEMBER 1937 — MONDAY
The rest of the hides were loaded. *Maroubra* will be back December 8th. Will start the camps up again and try and get a couple of hundred for her — very risky as storms coming on — might get away with it.

11 NOVEMBER 1937 — THURSDAY
Went to the station to do some work on the truck and to cart some fence posts.

12 NOVEMBER 1937 — FRIDAY
Working on the truck all day. All the natives here sick. There's a good few bush blacks about.

13 NOVEMBER 1937 — SATURDAY
Finished the truck and went over two miles of the fence line with the compass.

15 NOVEMBER 1937 — MONDAY
Finished carting the posts on to the plain and went back to the buffalo camps. Took Knight a ton of salt. Went to de Milles' camp.

1 DECEMBER 1937 — WEDNESDAY
Working around the station. No sign of de Milles. May have had a bad trip in. No road for the first forty miles and only a bridle pad after that. Stott who is supposed to come back to finish the saddling is about three weeks overdue.

3 DECEMBER 1937 — FRIDAY

Finished the fence this morning. After dinner a boy turned up
with a note from Jack Gaden saying he's very sick and asking
me to come down, so put the tyre chains on and started, plain
very boggy, went the first two miles in four hours. Gaden
down with malaria fever, dosed him with quinine.

4 DECEMBER 1937 — SATURDAY

Gaden very bad last night but took a turn for the better this
morning. Went over to the Wildman this morning and got
his mate Collins and brought him back.

5 DECEMBER 1937 — SUNDAY

Back to Ingarrabba. Ran over my dog Caesar and killed him.
Very sorry about it, he was a good mate.

7 DECEMBER 1937 — TUESDAY

Back to Kapalga for the boat that tied up just as I got there.
This is the last trip this year. No boats till March or April.

INGARRABBA
NORTHERN TERRITORY

7 DECEMBER 1937

Dear Mum

Received your letter with the newspaper cutting in it, by the
last *Maroubra*. It's extraordinary when you come to think of it!
You get news about the Territory quicker than I do.

When I was in Darwin buying my truck, Doctor Fenton
was lost and had been missing a couple of days. I didn't know he
had been found until the *Maroubra* got here on her last trip.
When I left Darwin he had been missing five days and everybody had given him up, although the search was still going
strong. He's always 'in the news'. He has crashed four planes,
but has never failed to get a patient in. When Fenton is called he
goes — day or night — and gets there. It's very rare that he has

an aerodrome to land on — it's a saying that Fenton could land in a horse-yard.

The bottom has dropped out of the buffalo hide market and I think I am going to be caught with a couple of hundred hides or perhaps more. When the slide started I had 150 on the way down to Sydney and I don't know how they got on. I have 138 going away on the December steamer and I am quite expecting to get a bill back for freight. But I've been expecting this, the price has been too good to last.

I don't know exactly what I'll be doing through the wet season. I've got so much to do that I don't know how to go about it. Just at present I have started fencing. I am going to do three miles for a start and I have a mile done. There are seven or eight miles to do altogether, and when it is finished I will have a good paddock that will hold 1000 head of bullocks easily.

Then there is a house to be built and the stockyard to be finished — there are 24 big heavy gates to be made for that! — and calves and foals to brand. Then I have 60 or 70 heifers to get from Goodparla Station, which I bought and paid for last year and, but for the Goodparla blokes making a mess of their muster, I would have had them delivered this year.

All my men, except one, have walked out on me. I have Jack Knight on the Wildman River. Stott, a man engaged to repair my gear (saddle, packs, collars), got mixed up in a lawsuit and had to go to Darwin as a witness, and he should have been back a fortnight ago.

I sent de Milles to Goodparla with my old truck and told him to leave it there and come back with horses. Cameron decided to go with him for the trip. I didn't mind because they should have been back in four days and that was ten days ago — God only knows where any of them are. I expect they decided to go to Pine Creek for the day (it's only 40 or 50 miles) and got caught by storms and are probably now back in Pine Creek in the D.T.s. By now I expect they've sold the truck and 'liquidated' the proceeds. I should have gone myself but thought it would be all right putting them up at Goodparla. However, I s'pose things will straighten themselves out eventually. I know this much — Cameron and de Milles will have to tell a pretty good tale to hold their jobs — I'm all ready to fire them out.

I should be out mustering horses now. I haven't had a horse muster this year and they have got a decent scatter on. However, I can't get away and leave the wet season's supply of rations to the tender mercies of the bush blacks.

I hope you get this before Xmas, but can't guarantee it. Anyhow, it's probably the last you'll hear of me 'til April or May next — if I'm not in a straitjacket!

I hope everybody is doing well.

Anyhow, I hope you all have a Happy Christmas and a prosperous New Year. This will be the first Christmas I've been financial.

With love to all, your loving son
P.S. Just received your October letter and will answer it later. *Maroubra* here with cargo. Don't know if the puddings are here or not — expect they are — thanks for everything.

9 DECEMBER 1937 — THURSDAY
Worked on the fence in the morning and cutting and carting timber for the house in the afternoon.

11 DECEMBER 1937 — SATURDAY
To Kapalga, Jack Gaden very sick. Sent a boy to Oenpelli Mission to wireless through to the Flying Doctor (Fenton). Collins (Gaden's mate) and will clear an aerodrome tomorrow.

12 DECEMBER 1937 — SUNDAY
Collins and I with a mob of blacks clearing a 'drome.

13 DECEMBER 1937 — MONDAY
Felling, digging out stumps and dragging. If Oenpelli can get through, Fenton should be here tomorrow at the latest.

14 DECEMBER 1937 — TUESDAY
Finished the drome and went back to the station, nothing more I can do at Kapalga. de Milles progressing well with my house.

15 DECEMBER 1937 — WEDNESDAY
Put the day in on the fence. Got a call from Kapalga to go and
tow their truck in, which is broken down out in the bush, so
went straight away, while there is a break in the weather.

16 DECEMBER 1937 — THURSDAY
Reached the truck just before daylight and as there was rain
about, hooked on and went straight back. Got into Kapalga
about midday. Flying Doctor been and gone. Went back to
the station.

25 DECEMBER 1937 — SATURDAY
All operations suspended for today. Ted Collins turned up
from Kapalga in time for dinner. No storms lately.

26 DECEMBER 1937 — SUNDAY
Everybody back on the job again today.

28 DECEMBER 1937 — TUESDAY
Another storm today. The fence finished and ready for the
wire to be strained.

29 DECEMBER 1937 — WEDNESDAY
House finished today but carted about twenty truck loads of
ant bed for the floor. I won't shift over until a kitchen has
been built.

31 DECEMBER 1937 — FRIDAY
Another year gone and a considerable amount of work done
— 1600 hides shot, a house built, a motor garage built, a
well sunk to 30 feet and equipped with windlass — 4 miles
of fence is nearly complete. The plant now consists of about
60 horses, ten riding saddles, six pack saddles, eight rifles, a
small blacksmith shop and two motor trucks. I have about
200/300 head of cattle. I am starting to see daylight but
there's plenty of work to be done yet.

1938

1 JANUARY 1938 — SATURDAY

The New Year blew in on a young cyclone with some heavy rain. Very satisfactory start. Cattle and all the horses, except three that are lost, are back here now. Plenty of feed and water everywhere. Dave built a substantial plum duff. Sid de Milles had a day off and I carted fencing wire and got some cedar logs to make furniture.

3 JANUARY 1938 — MONDAY

Finished the fence right through. Jack Knight arrived from the Wildman, where he is running a camp for me, to do up the station accounts and books. Will try and get away to Pine Creek tomorrow. Paid off most of the blacks. Drafted off a plant of horses for the road and got my packs ready. Will take two boys, seven horses and two packs.

6 JANUARY 1938 — THURSDAY

Went on this morning and reached Goodparla Station (now known as Gerowie). Stevens' stock camp here ready to leave for a bullock muster. Stevens offered the place to me cheap. Decided to put in a few days and inspect.

7 JANUARY 1938 — FRIDAY

Went out with the stock camp to Bunga Lookra Creek. Saw a lot of cattle with a good percentage of bullocks. Got two falls. The first time was caught in the iron and dragged and the second time yarding cattle my horse put his foot in a hole and turned over. Got knocked about a bit.

8 JANUARY 1938 — SATURDAY
Mustered Jacky's Creek. Got a good few cattle. Plenty of cleanskins and bullocks. Got another fall galloping and got the horse on top of me this time. Worst fall I've had for some time. Mustered in to the station.

10 JANUARY 1938 — MONDAY
Camped at the Nine Mile Yard. Practically decided to close. About eight hundred and forty square miles of well watered country carrying five to seven thousand head of cattle. Cattle very wild and out of hand, yards not of much use. Five years solid work straightening the place up.

George Stevens who owned Goodparla Station asked if I wanted to buy it, he'd sell it to me cheap. This gave me something to think about. I'd ridden through it many times on my way to Pine Creek and knew it quite well. It was so cheap I bought it.

18 JANUARY 1938 — TUESDAY
Darwin. I went to Lands and Surveys department to arrange for the transfer of the Goodparla (or Gerowie) lease.

20 JANUARY 1938 — THURSDAY
Everything is gradually being done. Land transfer completed today.

21 JANUARY 1938 — FRIDAY
Brands transferred today.

C/- COUSIN & CO
DARWIN

25 JANUARY 1938

Dear Mum

Received your last letter of November 27th when I got into Pine Creek after the New Year. I couldn't leave the place until January 4th and had to ride in with pack horses.

I think I told you in my last letter that I was considering buying a butchery business and a cattle station, however that deal didn't materialize. But I have bought a place called Goodparla — latterly the name has been changed to Gerowie — and I think it will be a good deal. There is about 840 square miles and is probably carrying about 5000 head of cattle or more. It is very difficult to estimate the size of the herd as it has been very much neglected and no proper records of brandings have been kept.

There are plenty of saleable bullocks on the place and the price of cattle has taken a slight rise. I am going straight back out there now, but won't be able to do any branding until after the wet season, but have plenty of work on the fences. I hope to be sending bullocks away by about June.

I hope to be selling bullocks and hides and am looking forward to a good year. I am in excellent health and everybody tells me how well I look. My ankle has completely recovered. As far as coming home in the winter goes, I wouldn't mind coming home any time, but would prefer the summer, however that is my busy time.

I got your Xmas parcel when I reached Pine Creek. I stay with the Stevens family when I'm in Pine Creek and they are very good friends to me. We all enjoyed a belated Xmas dinner.

When I am in Darwin I always stay at Fred Morris' place. I have been staying with them, when in Darwin, for six years now and am one of the family. Would you like to write to her? I know she would like to hear from you.

Must close now with love to everybody, your loving son

28 JANUARY 1938 — FRIDAY
Mick Madigan will come out to Goodparla with me, to do
some yard building. Boy riding a filly galloped into a tree
and broke his leg.

30 JANUARY 1938 — SUNDAY
Mick and I got away in the afternoon with 11 horses, six
packs and two boys, who will build stock yards.

2 FEBRUARY 1938 — WEDNESDAY
Reached the new station. Paddocked the horses and
straightened things up. I will have to go out for beef
tomorrow and after that will build a drafting yard.

15 FEBRUARY 1938 — TUESDAY
Pine Creek. Teeming rain all day. Heaviest wet we've had
since 1934. The Mary will be 4 miles wide at the crossing.

18 FEBRUARY 1938 — FRIDAY
General floods everywhere — no air mail as planes are all
grounded — Miles of telegraph lines washed away, right
into South Australia.

19 FEBRUARY 1938 — SATURDAY
Went to Darwin on the train as fed up with paddling round
Pine Creek.

23 FEBRUARY 1938 — WEDNESDAY
Back to Pine Creek by train. All creeks and rivers running
strong; no chance of getting out yet.

28 FEBRUARY 1938 — MONDAY
Countryside still a quagmire from the floods. Will try and
get out Monday or Tuesday. 32nd birthday.

3 MARCH 1938 — THURSDAY
Arrived station midday. Good deal of damage done here by

floods. Paddock fences swept away in several places. Lot of horses got away. Mick Madigan has done a good deal of work on the yard.

14 APRIL 1938 — THURSDAY
Packed up four packs of horses and took two boys and left for Ingarrabba to start the buffalo camps up.

16 APRIL 1938 — SATURDAY
Pushed on. Some of the creeks down here still running strong. Plenty of bog. When it got dark not quite sure of my whereabouts, so camped. Very close to the station.

17 APRIL 1938 — SUNDAY
Two miles to the station. Got there early. Note from Jack Knight saying he had left and had gone to Bill Black's buffalo camp to work. One hundred hides shot.

18 APRIL 1938 — MONDAY
Put in a day riding about. Cattle shifted over to the river. Horses not in very good condition. Three died during the wet.

21 APRIL 1938 — THURSDAY
Got to Goodparla Station about 8.30 a.m.

23 APRIL 1938 — SATURDAY
Handled a few colts. Drafted off horses for Mick Madigan to take away. He leaves in a day or two to start down to his buffalo camp.

GOODPARLA STATION
NORTHERN TERRITORY

25 APRIL 1938

Dear Peggy
Pleased and surprised to get your letter of February 17th. I'm sorry I haven't replied before, but I've been working like a

slave and am just having an enforced breather before rushing into a muster of my latest property.

I expect you are looking forward to me coming home and nobody is looking forward to it more than me — I am getting quite desperate. At times I feel quite fed up and would chuck it all in for very little. I have worked hard for years building things up. I have two stations that have an aggregate area of 1190 square miles. I have two trucks, several hundred head of horses (God knows what the exact number is), about 5000 head of cattle (conservative estimate), 16 riding saddles, 12 pack saddles, and all the gear and plant necessary to run a cattle station and buffalo camp.

My valuation of the whole lot is £5000. I'd sell for three probably couldn't get two. I could muster 500 saleable bullocks, which anywhere else would represent sound assets. Bullocks in Adelaide are selling up to £14 per head, but that's 2000 miles away! If I could get £4 per head within two hundred miles of the station, I could have a trip home once a year and God knows it's not much for a bullock. However, there is another side to all this — there is an old adage that says 'Buy in a slump and sell in a boom' — if the cattle industry had been flourishing I wouldn't have got this place for what I did. When I first came into the Pine Creek district bullocks were fetching £5 per head, and those times will probably come again. When the tide turns — I will be on top — if I can hang on!

My future largely depends on the government policy with regard to this country. They are beginning to take an interest in it and recently appointed a commission to enquire and report into the conditions and disabilities. This commission made a very sound report and recommended some sweeping changes. If the recommendations are adopted, everything will improve and the value of properties will increase four fold.

I am depending on the buffalo shooting to carry me through. The market is not so favourable this year as last year, but I've got to make it somehow. I'll cram 12 months of work into six and if there's a buffalo bull left in my neck of the woods, he won't be worth shooting.

I am writing this from Goodparla Station (also known as Gerowie). I have been here since the end of January working and I haven't branded a calf yet. I have, however, built three stockyards in various parts of the run. They are enormous affairs, the smallest of which will hold 500 head of cattle. I have also done a bit of horse mustering and broken in a few colts. All of this is just preliminary work before the mustering starts.

I am starting the stock-camp up May 1st and will stay here until June. Then I will have to go down to the other place (70 or 80 miles down the Alligator River) and start buffalo shooting. I will try and get a man to come and run this place for me as I have far too much on my hands to do it justice. When I have finished shooting in October or November, I will bring the buffalo shooting plant back here and try and get the place cleaned up a bit. There are anything up to 3000 head of cleanskins (unbranded cattle) here, but if I brand 1500 I will be doing pretty well.

To work this place properly I need six more stockyards and about ten miles of fencing.

When I'm about eighty I'll probably own some fine cattle stations with thousands of fine cattle and blood horses. I'll have a substantial income and leave a big fortune to some relatives I've never seen — perhaps — if I can get away for a trip now and then there won't be too much left, I bet. If I don't get away pretty soon I'll crack and leave it all to the blacks. If I could get away for one decent trip I could settle down to another five years work, and by that time I'd probably be independent. But I'm at a very critical stage in my chequered career and could easily bust and I wouldn't like to have to go through all the ground work of battling through again; so I'm going to give it a good go.

I'm sorry to hear of your heart trouble, and hope that you are fit again soon. I did not know that John had a daughter, but I knew that Hilda did. I have never heard the names of any of their wives or husbands or children. However, I am glad to hear that you are all presumably enjoying matrimonial bliss, I've no doubt it has its advantages.

Well, Peggy, you've no idea how much I want to come back and see you all, and I am going to make a determined effort to do so. To do it I have to make £2000 between now and the end of the year, and that doesn't sound much (if you say it quick).

So here's hoping, with love to all, your affectionate brother

12 MAY 1938 — THURSDAY
Went back to the station to start mustering.

13 MAY 1938 — FRIDAY
Got an early start and went across to Bull Yard. Got a few cattle on the way. Been a lot of cattle here a week ago but have shifted somewhere. Plenty of tracks about a week old.

15 MAY 1938 — SUNDAY
Mustered across to the Nine Mile. Got a few cattle. Will camp here and muster for a day or so.

17 MAY 1938 — TUESDAY
Three boys left last night. Leaves me too shorthanded to muster. Packed up and battled back to the station with what cattle I have in hand. One boy at station, will put him into the stock camp and try and carry on.

23 MAY 1938 — MONDAY
Mustered up the creek, got a good few branders but no bullocks. Missing a lot of cattle in the hills through being shorthanded, could do with another two or three hands.

25 MAY 1938 — WEDNESDAY
Branded forty calves. Cut out the bullocks and let the rest of the cattle go. Have thirty bullocks in hand now.

1 JUNE 1938 — WEDNESDAY
Mustered up Goodparla Creek. Plenty of cattle through here. All very wild. Have as many cattle in hand as we can

handle. Will have to return to station and brand up and get
away to the buffalo camp.

6 JUNE 1938 — MONDAY
Got away this morning with sixty bullocks, thirty-nine
horses and all the gear and plant. Camped at the old station
and yarded the bullocks.

7 JUNE 1938 — TUESDAY
Went on this morning to Kinkayli. Did a bit of work on the
yard to make it hold bullocks. This is the last yard. Will
have to watch tomorrow night.

8 JUNE 1938 — WEDNESDAY
Went down the river to Barramundi Junction and camped.
Watched the bullocks. Had the moon nearly all night and
had no trouble.

10 JUNE 1938 — FRIDAY
Reached Ingarrabba about midday. Had a look at the check
fence. Will have to do a bit of work on it down by the
lagoon.

11 JUNE 1938 — SATURDAY
Worked on the fence and made it safe. Will tail the bullocks
for a day or so until they get used to their new home.

28 JUNE 1938 — TUESDAY
New moon. Started with the truck and had a fair run. Had
to corduroy two creek crossings. Camped Wildman River.
Hundred hides here shot by Knight during the wet season.

30 JUNE 1938 — THURSDAY
Back to Wildman and loaded 55 hides — will cart them to
Adelaide River on the truck. Boys started shooting. Got an
early start and hit the trail for Adelaide River. This road not
been used this year; it is overgrown and obliterated in most

34 Downlands Ave
Worthing
April 26. 38.

My Dear Tom
    In your last short letter you did not say if you see
the copy of diary which at last I found time to do
also a letter enclosed was from Peg She has been with
me 3 months having to remain in bed owing to the state
of her heart + as I told you we took her to the Royal
Free Hospital to have the heart tracings taken which is a
quite new machine + only 3 Doctors in England understand
it + quite privately) She is suffering from what the Specialist
describes as a disappointment, + unfortunately I am afraid she
is not happy with Bill + added to this her inability to
get about + enjoy herself with him. they have a beautiful car
his mother paid for nearly £200 a very nice home, I cannot
of course say one word to her, She is very highly strung + goes
off the deep end for very little, the Dr says they should have
a family, which neither want, so I do feel that I have done
all I can now + badly need a rest myself which I intend to
have. especially as there is at present only Donald home Phil
is with Norman they have the shop quite near Vectis Rd
there you may remember we once lived She has become a
florist + seems to like it the hours a very long in Town.
Len has also found a job greasy + painty with a builder
quite near there also. he has been very tiresome but Norman
seems to be the only one that can manage him + I am
very glad indeed to pass on the responsibility.

places. Went bush on the McKinlay River; lost the track again at Angalara. Reached Adelaide River Siding 8.30 — 120 miles from Banana Creek.

2 JULY 1938 — SATURDAY
Train arrived an hour early. If it does this again it'll blow up.

6 JULY 1938 — WEDNESDAY
Turned the truck over this morning going round a sharp bend 10 miles from Darwin. Got some assistance and, with wire cables, blocks etc., got her back on her feet. Found the petrol line cut, so had to go to Darwin to get a new pipe.

7 JULY 1938 — THURSDAY
Fitted petrol pipe and brought the truck in to Darwin. Hides practically unsaleable.

8 JULY 1938 — FRIDAY
Wired Sydney regarding hides.

9 JULY 1938 — SATURDAY
Reply to wire, Sydney cabling London; will have to wait replies.

14 JULY 1938 — THURSDAY
Sold 150 hides to Jollys.

15 JULY 1938 — FRIDAY
Sold a further 500 hides to Jollys.

16 JULY 1938 — SATURDAY
Sold 500 hides to Cooper.

18 JULY 1938 — MONDAY
Got back to the camp at Banana Creek.

23 JULY 1938 — THURSDAY
Some poaching going on on the boundary. Think it is Vegas' camp getting in. Rode till nearly dark. Saw a camp fire across a swamp. Believe it is Vegas' shooting camp.

24 JULY 1938 — SUNDAY
Bill Black came across with me. Saw buffalo carcases on the plains. Black and I rode till dark and struck Vegas' main camp on the West Alligator.

25 JULY 1938 — MONDAY
Crossed the river and had a show down with Vegas. Returned to my camp. Black went back to his.

8 AUGUST 1938 — MONDAY
De Milles finished up today. Wound his camp up.

9 AUGUST 1938 — TUESDAY
Boat arrived. Took some loading off and put 220 hides on.

10 AUGUST 1938 — WEDNESDAY
Started with pack horses for Goodparla. Fin, Fred Hardy, myself, two boys and fifteen horses.

14 AUGUST 1938 — SUNDAY
Went to the station via Bungalookoa and the Nine Mile, saw about fifty to sixty head of cattle.

20 AUGUST 1938 — SATURDAY
Ingarrabba for dinner. Returned to the buffalo camp by truck.

I was beginning to think I was out of my mind buying Goodparla, when Fred Hardy turned up. He had sold his buffalo camp and cattle at Mount Bundy and moved to Perth, only to return disgruntled. On the spur of the moment I offered to sell him Goodparla and he took it.

C/- COUSIN & CO
DARWIN

28 AUGUST 1938

Dear Mum

Have just received your letter of August 6th, being in Darwin on business.

I have sold Goodparla and am trying to sell the other place now. I got £1000 for Goodparla in cash, but of course I had to release a stock mortgage as I bought on terms and had not paid for it. However, I have made a few hundred out of the deal, so can't complain. I didn't like letting it go as it was a good property and will be very valuable in a year or so. However, I couldn't carry the two places on as it was too much for me. I was trying to run both and really they were both being neglected. I have plenty of work to catch up on Ingarrabba, which should have been done last wet. I haven't branded a calf there yet and there is all of last year's calving to do yet, apart from other station work.

I had a breakdown with my truck and am at present waiting for it to be fixed up. Today is Sunday and I hope to get away back to the shooting early tomorrow morning. I am a long way behind this year. I have only got about 300 shot. I have contracted for 1150 but am afraid now that some of them will have to go short.

Love to all, your loving son

P.S. Mrs Morris received a letter from you and was very pleased about it. I am very glad you write to one another.

3 SEPTEMBER 1938 — SATURDAY

Out shooting — a bull turned back in the timber and nearly got my horse horned, lifted him right off his feet — rifle misfired. Put Jack Knight on.

14 SEPTEMBER 1938 — WEDNESDAY

Reached Adelaide River, went on out by Marrakia Station and camped at Mary River. Fred Hardy with me, on his way

to take delivery of the Goodparla plant and take possession
of the station.

16 SEPTEMBER 1938 — FRIDAY
Fred Hardy took delivery of 14 horses from the Goodparla
plant. Arranged to give him delivery at the station on the
21st. No shooting today.

17 SEPTEMBER 1938 — SATURDAY
Out shooting. Stott over from Bill Black's camp claiming all
hides in the camp on behalf of Black, also notice to shift
camp. They are not recognizing claims, so I'm asking for a
survey.

18 SEPTEMBER 1938 — SUNDAY
Stott left for the telegraph line to wire Black for instruction.

20 SEPTEMBER 1938 — TUESDAY
Took 31 hides to the landing and went on to station and met
Fred Hardy, to give him delivery of the Goodparla plant and
horses.

29 SEPTEMBER 1938 — THURSDAY
Shifted back to the main camp and ran another load of hides
to landing. Left two boys to load up the *Maroubra*.

30 SEPTEMBER 1938 — FRIDAY
Left with a load of hides for Darwin and to consult Foster
regarding boundary dispute. Lights fused. Drove until the
moon set and got within 25 miles of Darwin — 160 mile run.

6 OCTOBER 1938 — THURSDAY
Left Darwin this morning. Late start. Dinner at Adelaide
River siding (77 miles). Camped at Scott's Creek (another 60
miles). Picked up Sandy McNab of the police, who is on
patrol out my way. Piloted him out.

8 OCTOBER 1938 — SATURDAY
Stott, Black's overseer and McNab came back to my camp in
connection with the boundary dispute. Matters are at a
deadlock and I'm not going to budge an inch. Reported loss
of pack saddle. McNab and Stott left.

11 OCTOBER 1938 — TUESDAY
Sent the plant straight across country to Gypsy Spring with
the boys. Dave and myself went to Kapalga to clean up
aerodrome for Roy Edwards, who may come out tomorrow
with mail.

12 OCTOBER 1938 — WEDNESDAY
Put the finishing touches to the aerodrome this morning. Ran
up to the station for a look around. Somebody has been
through and killed a bullock on the road. Only about ten
days of water left. Will have to shift cattle shortly. No plane
— left a note and went down to the spring.

14 OCTOBER 1938 — FRIDAY
Ran down to Mangulla in the truck for a look around. All
the waters down here have dried up and the buffalo have
shifted. Bush fire went through the camp and destroyed a lot
of stuff and damaged about a ton and a half of salt.

20 OCTOBER 1938 — THURSDAY
Got on to a patch of buffalo today. Ten hides. Should get a
hundred hides quick and lively out of this neck of the woods.

23 OCTOBER 1938 — SUNDAY
Storms starting now.

29 OCTOBER 1938 — SATURDAY
Bill Black ran me back to my camp in his truck. Arranged to
shoot 150 hides on his country and pay him a royalty of 4
shillings per hide. Will see Black, November 2nd at his
camp.

25 NOVEMBER 1938 — FRIDAY
Maroubra due today. Couple of good storms. Unusual amount
of rain for this time of the year. Arranged with Dodson to
put up 5 miles of fence.

C/- COUSIN & CO
DARWIN N.T.
AUSTRALIA

25 NOVEMBER 1938

Dear Uncle

I received your letter of October 18th on November 10th
while on the Wildman River where I had been shooting,
which is pretty good going. It came out on the auxiliary ketch
Wanderer.

Well I'm not the landowner I was. I sold Goodparla but still
have the other place, Ingarrabba.

You don't know what a scandalous train service is until
you've been to the Northern Territory. We've got one railway
line here and one train, 'Leaping Lena'. It goes once a week and
it is quite an event along the line. If you know the guard and
driver you don't have to pay your fare, but you're expected to
cut the money out in beer, which although it isn't saving
anything, makes the journey interesting. The guard is a champ
at hitting telegraph poles with bottles, empty ones when the
train is in motion, which when downhill with a following wind
does 30. I took him on once, betting bottles of beer and
doubling up — I thought the first few were flukes — it cost me
two dozen to find out they weren't.

Don't talk to me about hospitals. I had enough of them
when I was in for 11 weeks. I drank everything from Epsom
Salts to Soligmum (*a white ant deterrent*) and nearly got my taste
for beer ruined. I'm pretty right now though, but I don't get
much chance out here for beer. I've got a friend with a plane
and I'm getting him to come out to the station for Christmas
with half a dozen on ice. Never been done before on the

Alligator River. I suppose ice is a thing you don't look for about Christmas time.

Well all the best for the festive season.

With love to auntie, your affectionate reply

C/- COUSIN & CO
DARWIN N.T.

25 NOVEMBER 1938

Dear Peg

Yours of the 12th reached me about a fortnight ago on the Wildman River, where I was shooting.

Very interested in your description of the war precautions. I don't think anybody out here realised how serious it is. Most of us know in a vague sort of way that something was on in Czechoslovakia.

There are wireless sets here and there, so the news filters through. In Darwin there are planes pretty well every day and they are abreast of the news. Up country, however, it is different. There is only one train a week and it only potters out 400 miles, which is as far as it can go. From where I am shooting it is only 150 miles to the line, but I don't go in any oftener than I can help. I put most of the road through myself and it's pretty awful. My truck, a big two ton V8, is only 12 months old and it looks 12 years; this country is what tanks and tractors were made for, not cars. Of course, I turned it over once with 35 cwt of hides on her and that didn't improve it.

I suppose you are all wondering when I am going to come home for a trip. I don't know myself, although I feel that I need a holiday badly. I've been getting very crotchety lately.

I have a good deal of branding to do. I haven't branded a calf here for two years. There are some big cleanskins running around asking for a branding iron. If I don't put the Rising Sun (the station brand) on them, somebody else will put something else on 'em. I am putting a five mile extension on my check fence. So, with a few other jobs, I have my hands full for a good while.

I have had a hell of a lot of rain here this month. It is rather early, but I've been expecting it because the last three seasons have been light. The water hole at the homestead went dry two years in succession and I had to shift all the cattle and horses. Of course, we have a well for our own use.

Anyhow, the rain we've been getting lately has made good surface water everywhere, but I've had a hell of a time carting hides. I got bogged on a plain and a storm came up and I had to leave my truck there all night and in the morning it was in three feet of water!

I've been living in bog lately. I dream about it and wake up screaming. I carry chains, wire ropes, pulleys, levers, Kangaroo Jack, not to mention shovels and axes. When that big brute of a truck of mine runs into soft ground she's in her glory. She just dives straight down and doesn't pull up till the diff is buried.

I had to knock off shooting a bit earlier and I thought for a while I wouldn't be able to get my hides to the landing. However, we got a break for a day or so and I managed to plough in with them. I'll send you some photos later. I've got some that'll make your hair stand on end.

Well all the best for Xmas and love to everybody.

Your affectionate brother

27 NOVEMBER 1938 — SUNDAY
New moon. *Maroubra* arrived. Half my loading left in Darwin, so I will have to go in. Loading 115 hides. Left Dodson in charge and left with the *Marboubra* for Darwin.

3 DECEMBER 1938 — SATURDAY
Left with Roy Edwards by plane for the station, and did the run in an hour and a half. Made a good landing on the edge of the lagoon.

4 DECEMBER 1938 — SUNDAY
Had a look at the country through which the proposed new 5 mile fence line will run.

5 DECEMBER 1938 — MONDAY
Started to run the line and clear it. Did about 2 miles. Four
boys clearing an aerodrome.

8 DECEMBER 1938 — THURSDAY
Big day. Got busy with the soldering iron and about five
pounds of solder and made a petrol funnel. Snowy, out post
cutting, brought one boy in unconscious — some kind of a
stroke.

17 DECEMBER 1938 — SATURDAY
Out on the fence line.

18 DECEMBER 1938 — SUNDAY
Day of rest.

25 DECEMBER 1938 — SUNDAY
Had a shave.

26 DECEMBER 1938 — MONDAY
Boat due today. Snowy took some boys and did some
clearing on the new aerodrome.

27 DECEMBER 1938 — TUESDAY
If the boat doesn't come today, it won't come at all. Will
give it a few days and then will have to do something as will
be short of rations and the natives' tobacco soon — feeding
17. Cross branded some horses. Got kicked.

28 DECEMBER 1938 — WEDNESDAY
Snowy took most of the boys and went back onto the line of
fence — decided to run it to the Two Mile Billabong —
about seven miles, about 2000 posts to cut altogether. Self
working on the drafting yard at the station. A good deal of
work to be done to it.

1939

1 JANUARY 1939 — SUNDAY
Snowy Dodson returned from line of fence. All the posts are cut and laid on the line.

3 JANUARY 1939 — TUESDAY
Went out with the boys to muster and brand up the cattle, before we get any more heavy rain.

9 JANUARY 1939 — MONDAY
Mild epidemic of dengue fever.

10 JANUARY 1939 — TUESDAY
A day's spell. Some boys went for a walkabout. Put some new ones on. Rainy.

12 JANUARY 1939 — THURSDAY
Packed a couple of boys off to Oenpelli Mission to radio to Darwin to try and get Roy Edwards to fly out and bring some stores, and also to find out something about the rest of my stores that the *Maroubra* left in Darwin by mistake in November. Will be very short before long.

15 JANUARY 1939 — SUNDAY
Gate making. Drizzling rain. English flying boat passed at 100 feet high — visibility bad for flying.

27 JANUARY 1939 — FRIDAY

Finished the yard today with the exception of capping the
gateways. Will have to wait for the fencing camp as the gate
caps are about 4 cwt each. Three more gates to make.

28 JANUARY 1939 — SATURDAY

Gave the boys working here a day's spell and rode out and
had a look at the fence.

INGARRABBA
NORTHERN TERRITORY

28 JANUARY 1939

. . . Well the *Wanderer* hasn't turned up to date and the supplies
are getting low. On 12 January I sent a boy to Oenpelli Mission,
about 40 or 50 miles, with a radio to Darwin. He could have
been back in a week, but it is now getting on for three weeks
with no sign of him. I am getting through a lot of work just now
and consequently, I am feeding a lot of natives. There are 14
natives and Snowy Dodson and myself — three feeds a day —
and a lot of rations are necessary.

Since I came back from Darwin I have completed the cattle
yards at the station, the necessary additions taking 290 rails and
78 posts. Four miles of fence is up (another three to do), and an
aerodrome, 450 yards by 100 yards, cleared and grubbed; this
last is no mean feat.

Christmas here was just another day, chiefly remarkable
for the fact that I had a shave. I've got a chap named Dodson
working here and we cracked a bottle of rum — 'A Merry
Xmas', I said as we tossed a noggin down — it sounded idiotic.

Only about half my wet season loading came out on the last
trip of the coastal launch *Maroubra* — she came out on 28th
November for my last load of hides — so I decided I'd better go
into Darwin. So I hopped on the *Maroubra* and went back with
her. I found the rest of the load was still in the bond, so I made
arrangements for the ketch *Wanderer* to bring it out.

I returned to the station by plane. A friend of mine who has a pearling fleet operating from Darwin has just bought a plane and we came out here in an hour and a half. It takes five days with packhorses to get to Adelaide River (the railway line) and it takes two days in the truck. It is 105 air miles from Darwin to the station, over what I judge to be rotten flying country — all bush, heavily timbered and no townships or habitations of any description.

Roy had never flown over here before and he thought we might get bushed, so he took plenty of benzine. I was pretty confident, but Roy said I wouldn't recognise the country from the air — it looks so different.

Well we took off about 7.30 a.m. We were just clear of the trees when we passed over Mrs Morris standing in the garden waving to me, the dear old soul. I gave her a good wave, but don't know whether she could see me as we were travelling so fast. I haven't seen her since, so write and ask her. Anyhow, we had a wonderful trip and I had no trouble keeping Roy on a perfect course.

I don't think we lost a mile in the 105. We hit the station dead centre. We weren't quite sure about landing. There is an aerodrome at Kapalga, seven miles north of my homestead (I cleared it last year for the Flying Doctor when a chap was sick). However I thought we might be able to land at the homestead on the edge of the lagoon, which is dry, and failing that we could go to Kapalga and land. (I had arranged for Dodson to send horses down for me if he saw the plane didn't land.) Anyhow, Roy had a good look at it and decided to give it a go — made a perfect landing. I was sorry when the trip was over. I took some photos of the plane with the station boys and lubras and also killed a bullock and sent some beef back to Mrs Morris. I do hope she got it all right.

2 FEBRUARY 1939 — THURSDAY
Fence finished midday today. Worked out to be over six miles. Still gate making. Sent pack horses out to shift the fencing camp in, too boggy and wet for the truck.

4 FEBRUARY 1939 — SATURDAY
Finished the sixth stockyard gate, thank God. Have to be
bolted together now and swung. Geese starting to lay. Boys
brought eggs in today.

12 FEBRUARY 1939 — SUNDAY
Working on paddock. Boy returned from Oenpelli, he's been
away exactly a month. No reply to radio. Gave the reply to
another boy who might be another month.

16 FEBRUARY 1939 — THURSDAY
Repairing harness saddles etc. when boy arrived with radio
message. I can't make head nor tail of it.

17 FEBRUARY 1939 — FRIDAY
Will have to try and get in to the telegraph line but I'm not
looking forward to the trip as all the rivers are up. Mustered
a plant and got my packs ready. Will take Frank and six
horses.

18 FEBRUARY 1939 — SATURDAY
Got away after dinner, rained all the morning. Camped
West Alligator. Swam across.

20 FEBRUARY 1939 — MONDAY
Got on to ridgy country today. The going a lot better. Bog
in patches.

21 FEBRUARY 1939 — TUESDAY
Pushed on this morning. Hit Chachara range and had a
rough time getting through it. Camped close to the Mary
River, can hear it roaring, bad river to swim.

22 FEBRUARY 1939 — WEDNESDAY
Went over on to the Mary River this morning. Will follow
it up to the Pine Creek road. Struck the Little Mary coming
in from the east. Horses got swept down stream trying to

cross and everything got wet. Lit a fire and dried things out best I could. Packed up and went on up the river to the Pine Creek road crossing. Made a boat with pack saddles and tarpaulin and crossed everything. Swam horses. Camped Evelyn Silver Mine.

23 FEBRUARY 1939 — THURSDAY
Pine Creek 28 miles. Good road all the way. Took things easy, arrived about 4 p.m.

16 MARCH 1939 — THURSDAY
Darwin. Went aboard the *Violet*, left about 10.30 a.m. and anchored Pussy Cat Island.

20 MARCH 1939 — MONDAY
Went on up the river. Passed the station landing in a blinding storm and went back. Reached station about 10 a.m. All the boys except two left for a walkabout yesterday. Sent after them. Lubra taken by alligator three days ago.

21 MARCH 1939 — TUESDAY
Unloaded the *Violet* and got some of the stores over to the station.

28 MARCH 1939 — TUESDAY
About 7 o'clock, every boy and lubra on the place cleared out. Didn't discover it until they'd been gone fully an hour. Later on discovered lots of stores etc. missing.

29 MARCH 1939 — WEDNESDAY
Got away before daylight to track the natives, but they've got a big start on me. They must have travelled nearly all night. Went about 25 or 30 miles and lost their tracks on Bamboo Creek. Camped for the night — miserable camp — millions of mosquitos and nothing to eat, except for a handful of dried fruit, since yesterday.

30 MARCH 1939 — THURSDAY
Got back to the station about 4.30 this afternoon.

7 APRIL 1939 — FRIDAY
Got a plant ready to go into the telegraph line. Will take
Snowy Dodson in and go to Brocks Creek to make a report
to police. Left old Jimmy and Nellie at Kapalga to wait for
the *Maroubra* and look after the loading.

8 APRIL 1939 — SATURDAY
Got away this morning. Went as far as the West Alligator
and all the horses plunged into the river. Everything wet,
flour, tea, sugar, matches, swags, etc. Tried to dry things out
at the dinner camp and it came on to rain. Trying to dry the
sugar out, the bag got burnt. The only thing that isn't wet is
the baking powder and that's in a tin.

10 APRIL 1939 — MONDAY
Reached Goodparla Station. Mustering camp here.
Musterer's away. Still drying the camp out. Packs and
saddles heavy and sodden. The lid came off the baking
powder tin and we lost the lot.

14 APRIL 1939 — FRIDAY
To Brocks Creek. Caught the police officer in charge just as
he was off to Darwin. Will do a patrol for me but can't get
out for a week or so. Will wait for him.

22 APRIL 1939 — SATURDAY
To Tipperary Station to put the time in and try and buy
horses.

5 MAY 1939 — FRIDAY
Brocks Creek Police Patrol delayed, can't get away for
several weeks. Will have to go out to the station and meet
him there.

10 MAY 1939 — WEDNESDAY

Reached Old Goodparla Station. Fred Hardy camped here and tells me a couple of my horses are in the paddock. He suggests we ride over together tomorrow.

11 MAY 1939 — THURSDAY

I sold a mare to Fred Hardy and took a chestnut colt. Have 14 horses with me now. Went on and camped at the Alligator River crossing, on the Arnhem Land Mine Road. Charlie Payne, a buffalo shooter, also camped here with a plant of horses on his way down to shoot.

12 MAY 1939 — FRIDAY

Pushed on this morning. Camped Yemelba Spring. Sergeant and Madigan's truck bogged. Got the first definite news of my blacks. All down at Sergeant and Madigan's buffalo camp.

20 MAY 1939 — SATURDAY

Reached the Ingarrabba Station fairly early. Got the truck out and started for Stevens' camp. Only got a couple of miles and got hopelessly bogged in the middle of the plain. Worked till sundown but couldn't get it out. I had nothing to eat all day. I walked seven miles to Kapalga. Got mail left by *Maroubra*. Boat due back for hides July 6th or 7th.

23 MAY 1939 — TUESDAY

Went down to the Kapalga landing. Stevens and I checked the loading left by the *Maroubra*. Big shortage of stuff. The natives that I left here gone and probably taken some stuff with them.

24 MAY 1939 — WEDNESDAY

To Stevens' camp. Thirty-nine horses in hand all told, counting three of Stevens'.

25 MAY 1939 — THURSDAY

Stevens and boys out shooting. Self rigging a camp.

9 JUNE 1939 — FRIDAY
Bobby, my crack shooting horse, fell with me. First time
he's fallen I think.

12 JUNE 1939 — MONDAY
Took three boys to build a jetty at Kapalga. The old jetty
swept away in a flood. Left the boys cutting timber.

23 JUNE 1939 — FRIDAY
Good shooting. Horse called Trinket fell with George
Stevens and either broke or dislocated her shoulder. Had to
leave her out on the plain about three miles from the camp.

24 JUNE 1939 — SATURDAY
George took a couple of canteens of water and gave Trinket
a drink. Shoulder not too bad. Knee badly swelled.

6 JULY 1939 — THURSDAY
Started over to the lower Wildman Landing, had to
corduroy a salt water arm. Went on across the plain and had
to make a crossing in a creek and put another corduroy
down. Got bogged. Unloaded hides and returned to the
camp.

7 JULY 1939 — FRIDAY
Loaded up with hides and made another start for the
Wildman. Got bogged on the plain and had to unload. Got
bogged again in the first creek and had to unload again.
Went on to within a couple of miles of the landing and got
bogged again in heavy sand. Unloaded and returned to the
camp.

8 JULY 1939 — SATURDAY
Took the last load of dry hides from the camp this morning
and went straight through to the Wildman without any
trouble. Picked up the hides that I left on the sand yesterday.

22 JULY 1939 — SATURDAY
Carted another load of hides to the landing. No *Maroubra* yet,
a fortnight overdue. Will have to go to Darwin and find out
what is the hold up.

24 JULY 1939 — MONDAY
Left early this morning for Darwin. Took thirty hides.

25 JULY 1939 — TUESDAY
Reached Darwin. Hear the *Maroubra* is taken off the coast
and is going to New Guinea. Will have to make
arrangements for another boat.

27 JULY 1939 — THURSDAY
Made arrangements for the lugger *Venture* to go out and pick
my hides up.

4 AUGUST 1939 — FRIDAY
Front tyre blew out this morning. Reached the camp late in
the afternoon. Country shot out. Will move the camp as
soon as possible.

5 AUGUST 1939 — WEDNESDAY
Doing a bit of shooting round the camp waiting for boat to
turn up.

9 AUGUST 1939 — WEDNESDAY
Boat turned up this morning, loaded.

21 AUGUST 1939 — MONDAY
Put a day in on the track. Cleaned out the petrol tank. Will
make a start for Darwin tonight for a new radiator. Got
away fairly late. Went 8 miles and camped. Carburettor still
giving trouble.

22 AUGUST 1939 — TUESDAY
Went on and got stuck in the Mary River Crossing. Camped at Coolibah.

23 AUGUST 1939 — WEDNESDAY
Went on to Adelaide River. There is talk of war with Germany, which will mean the collapse of the hide market.

24 AUGUST 1939 — THURSDAY
Darwin after a bad day's run.

25 AUGUST 1939 — FRIDAY
Wired Farmers and Graziers regarding hide market.

26 AUGUST 1939 — SATURDAY
Mediterranean closed to shipping. This means the end of the hide market as all the buffalo hides go there.

28 AUGUST 1939 — MONDAY
Reply from Farmers and Graziers. Hide market collapsed.

29 AUGUST 1939 — TUESDAY
War seems to be unavoidable, will have to wait and see how things are going to go.

3 SEPTEMBER 1939 — SUNDAY
Left Darwin for Adelaide River. War declared.

9 SEPTEMBER 1939 — SATURDAY
Got a contract to shoot another 200 hides. Very poor price.

20 SEPTEMBER 1939 — WEDNESDAY
Secured a further 300 hide contract, total 500, 4 pence per pound.

30 SEPTEMBER 1939 — SATURDAY
Three boys and a lubra left last night. Stole some clothes and

rations on their way through. Charlie Payne at the station on his way down to see me. Offered him a job.

14 OCTOBER 1939 — SATURDAY
Went out with the shooters today and livened things up. Twenty-five hides. Had to get the truck to get the hides into the camp.

20 OCTOBER 1939 — FRIDAY
Charlie Payne's shooting horse dropped dead with him this morning.

31 OCTOBER 1939 — TUESDAY
Branded 249 hides and stacked them. Fixed up the jetty. Went up to the station in the evening to pick up a load of alligator hides.

8 NOVEMBER 1939 — WEDNESDAY
Returned to Kapalga. Boat turned up this afternoon. Loaded half the hides.

In 1939 I became MRO 3, which stood for Military Reporting Officer Number 3, attached to the Intelligence Section of the 7th Military District.

C/- GREGORY & CO
DARWIN

10 NOVEMBER 1939

Dear Mum

I have just received your letter and have time to scribble a line. A lugger is here taking a load of hides away. I have sold a few at a very low price, so I had to keep going.

I am very glad to hear you have shifted to Wales, the best thing you could do.

God only knows when the war will end or where we shall all be before then. I may possibly be dragged in later but am not looking forward to it. We know there is a war on all right, on account of Darwin being a garrison town.

We have all the services ably represented in Darwin. It is one of the most important places in Australia. All the Darwin mail is censored, I understand. Cattle prices are rising; they are pretty good now and will undoubtedly boom. Unfortunately, I haven't enough cattle to make more than a bare living out of it, but I may be able to get hold of some cheaply. I am thinking of negotiating for a property that is on the market, which is stocked with cattle, but I will have to raise some money somewhere. I think I can do that, all right.

Will close now as the *Venture* is leaving on the next tide. Don't worry any more than you can help. I don't think this war will last provided Russia keeps out, but it's very difficult to prophesy. My love to Auntie Em, Phil and Kath and of course yourself.

Your affectionate son.
P.S. I wrote to you C/- Uncle Tom as I didn't know your address.

14 NOVEMBER 1939 — TUESDAY
Back to the main camp. Started Ernest, the saddle boy, repairing the gear — saddles, packs, etc. — seems an eternal job.

3 DECEMBER 1939 — SUNDAY
Finished the yard. Back to the buffalo camp. Shooting finished — 500 hides.

20 DECEMBER 1939 — WEDNESDAY
Took a plant of horses and the boys and went across to the Wildman Plains on a horse mustering expedition.

23 DECEMBER 1939 — SATURDAY
Camped on Cattle Creek on the boundary. Decided to go
over and look Bill Black up.

24 DECEMBER 1939 — SUNDAY
To Stuart Station, Bill Black's place. His lugger the *Rozelle* is
overdue.

25 DECEMBER 1939 — MONDAY
Very 'dry' Christmas — Bill Black short of rations on
account of his boat being overdue. Ted White is coming on
the boat to do a few days' work on Black's truck. I will stay
and try and get him to come over to my place.

30 DECEMBER 1939 — SATURDAY
Left to go back. No boat — looks serious — *Rozelle* supposed
to have left Darwin — a two day trip usually. Left a boy to
bring word over provided the boat turns up in a week; boy
to stay no longer.

1940–1943

1 JANUARY 1940 — MONDAY
I returned to the station from Bill Black's place. Payne
returned from the Pine Creek trip, left the stores and mail
etc. and went back to his own camp. He lost a horse that I'd
lent him. Rained in the afternoon.

3 JANUARY 1940 — WEDNESDAY
Worked on the aerodrome in the morning, cutting light
growth. Some bush blacks turned up. Rained all the
afternoon — most promising wet I've seen since 1934.

11 JANUARY 1940 — THURSDAY
Sunny day. Started work on an engineer shop. Alec, the boy
I left at Black's place, returned with note — Bill Black's
lugger 16 days overdue and he fears she is lost.

23 JANUARY 1940 — TUESDAY
Left the station after dinner. Hit the West Alligator River
sundown. Water is bank to bank.

26 JANUARY 1940 — FRIDAY
Swam an outer channel of the river and camped.

27 JANUARY 1940 — SATURDAY
Went on this morning. Had to swim another channel and
later the Coirwong Creek.

29 JANUARY 1940 — MONDAY
Arrived Goodparla (now called Gerowie) Station early this
morning. Fred Hardy is in Darwin with a broken leg.

31 JANUARY 1940 — WEDNESDAY
Reached Pine Creek this morning.

1 FEBRUARY 1940 — THURSDAY
Sent my horses out to one of George Murray's paddocks on
Esmeralda Station.

2 FEBRUARY 1940 — FRIDAY
Pine Creek waiting for train.

3 FEBRUARY 1940 — SATURDAY
Train to Darwin.

12 FEBRUARY 1940 — MONDAY
Made an offer to G. J. Murray's solicitor for Esmeralda
Station and Butchery, Pine Creek.

15 FEBRUARY 1940 — THURSDAY
Wire came back from Sydney accepting offer.

16 FEBRUARY 1940 — FRIDAY
Arranged with bank for overdraft.

24 FEBRUARY 1940 — SATURDAY
Bill Black in from Stuart Station. He made me an offer for
one of my blocks on the Wildman River.

26 FEBRUARY 1940 — MONDAY
Accepted Black's offer for the Wildman block (100 square
miles).

28 FEBRUARY 1940 — WEDNESDAY
Train to Pine Creek to take possession. J. Peters in charge of

butchery. I left him in charge and W. Riley running stock-
camp, and made no alteration there, either. 34th birthday.

8 MARCH 1940 — FRIDAY

Peters down to it with malaria. Roy Edwards and Doctor
Fenton came in Fenton's moth. They are on their way to
Hodgson Downs to get Fenton's big plane, which he crashed
last week. They had an undercarriage and prop with them.
Sent hides to Darwin.

PINE CREEK

15 MARCH 1940

Dear Mum

Since writing to you last I have bought another property, a
place called Esmeralda Station with a butchery attached to it.
The butchery is in Pine Creek and the station runs out towards
the Mary River.

There are altogether six leases that all join one another and
have a total area of 700 square miles, or to be exact 711. There are
about 3000 head of cattle and a large number of horses, although
most of the horses are out of hand and pretty wild. The butchery
is quite a good little turnout, being quite self-contained. I have
my own slaughter-yard and all the necessary plant, including a
refrigerator, which will take four or five bullocks at a time.

I am putting five bullocks a week through the shop, and a
pig or so. I have a chap coming to manage the butchery part of
the business. I don't know enough about butchering to be able
to run it, and I will have to get out on the run pretty soon and
start branding calves. This is a mining district, although, just at
present, the mines are pretty dead. After the wet, however,
some of them will probably get a go on, which will probably
mean another bullock or so a week.

I have been here a fortnight and am pretty busy getting
things in order. I will have to be pretty careful for a while. I am
well into the bank over this turnout, but I am selling 750 head of

mixed cattle in May, which should put me on the right side of things. Must close now.

Love to all

16 MARCH 1940 — SATURDAY
Killed a red bullock branded G.M.T. Sent the stock-camp out to Esmeralda. Will have to get some bullocks for the shop and then get into some yard building. Will follow out on Monday. Fred Stevens took over the butchery and will manage the place for me.

18 MARCH 1940 — MONDAY
Left to join the stock camp at the station, seven miles out. Have about twenty bullocks to get for the shop before Thursday. Only three in hand.

26 MARCH 1940 — TUESDAY
Started cutting rails and posts for yard repair job. Good deal of work to be done here.

10 APRIL 1940 — WEDNESDAY
Went to Esmeralda and camped.

18 APRIL 1940 — THURSDAY
Shoeing horses. Got rations ready to start mustering.

23 APRIL 1940 — TUESDAY
Mustered up Boomerlura and Union Creek. Got about seventy head of cattle.

The mustering procedure and the number of cattle handled in a morning's muster would not vary very much. The afternoons were set aside for the drafting off of the fats. When the drafting was finished the rest of the mob was allowed to wander off and the bullocks were yarded. As the number of bullocks increased beyond what could be comfortably yarded they would have to be watched instead.

N° 4519

COMMONWEALTH OF AUSTRALIA.
The Northern Territory.

FEE - - FIVE SHILLINGS PER ANNUM.

Date of Issue *21st June, 1940*   Mining District *9*

Place of Issue *Darwin*

Miner's Right

Issued to *Thomas Ernest Cole* of *Pine Creek*

under the provisions of the *Northern Territory Mining Act* 1903, to be in force until *Twentieth*

day of *June,*   1944, and available for *Northern Territory*

W. a. Hughes.
Chief Warden.

By Authority: L. F. JOHNSTON, Commonwealth Government Printer, Canberra.

---

26 APRIL 1940 — FRIDAY

Shifted camp across to Francis. Got about thirty head of cattle. Got to Francis Yard late and lost a few cattle yarding in the dark. Self sick with severe cold and touch of fever.

2 MAY 1940 — THURSDAY

Cattle rushed just before daylight this morning and smashed the yard. Put in nearly all day tracking them. Got most of them.

18 MAY 1940 — SATURDAY

Shifted to Douglas yard, about 250 head of cattle in hand. This yard is small and not too strong. Will have to take a hundred into Pine Creek tomorrow to relieve it.

19 MAY 1940 — SUNDAY

To Pine Creek with cattle. Left one boy tailing 150 head of cattle. Riley mustering. Returned and found boy had gone bush and let 150 head of cattle go.

20 MAY 1940 — MONDAY
Got some of the cattle lost yesterday, not many, about
eighty or ninety, still going.

26 MAY 1940 — SUNDAY
Left Esmeralda.

30 MAY 1940 — THURSDAY
Arranged for Yorky Billy to go over to Kapalga Station and
take charge for me. Left him a horse and pack.

31 MAY 1940 — FRIDAY
Arrived Ingarrabba Station. Everything more or less right.
Got verification of murder of Michael. Speared five or six
times by few boys. All very nonchalant about it.

11 JUNE 1940 — TUESDAY
Went on to Pine Creek. Mustering plant here. 136 calves
been branded.

15 JULY 1940 — MONDAY
Cattle very wild here. Got six head. Two jumped out of the yard.

23 JULY 1940 — TUESDAY
Branded 39 calves. 18 males, 21 females. Sent the bullocks into Pine Creek.

10 OCTOBER 1940 — THURSDAY
Reached Ingarrabba Station early this morning. Turned all the horses out on to good feed.

11 OCTOBER 1940 — FRIDAY
Mustered horses and left for a ride around and a muster. Camped Kapalga (old station). Eschelby's boat at landing taking in water. Says Harry Hardy got killed at Adelaide River Races.

15 OCTOBER 1940 — TUESDAY
Repairing fences. Mustering horses etc.

29 OCTOBER 1940 — TUESDAY
Left with 18 fats [fat cattle] for Pine Creek. Camped Red Lily. Watched the cattle all night, gave no trouble.

30 OCTOBER 1940 — WEDNESDAY
On to Noel Hall's camp. Hall mustering. Hall says Fred Hardy got killed at the races not Harry. He was riding a horse he called Goodparla Gold in one of the races and it fell with him and killed him.

3 NOVEMBER 1940 — SUNDAY
Across to the Mary River. Got bushed going across and didn't reach the yard till dark and found it had been burnt by a bush fire. Watched cattle all night.

N° 144

SMT

Q

NEAR

CODE A 5

THE NORTHERN TERRITORY OF AUSTRALIA.

Brands Ordinance 1928-1934.
Regulation 21 (3).   Form M.

CERTIFICATE OF TRANSFER OF BRAND.

THIS IS TO CERTIFY *that the Brands and Earmark mentioned hereunder were this day*
transferred from George John Murray

of

to Thomas Ernest Cole

of

for use on Esmeralda Station, Pine Creek *Run or Holding.*

Dated this 29 *day of* June 19 40

L. Twendale
Deputy   *Registrar of Brands.*

FEE: £0 10 0

---

6 NOVEMBER 1940 — WEDNESDAY
On to Pine Creek and delivered bullocks. Light storm.

29 NOVEMBER 1940 — FRIDAY
Darwin. Made application for Kapalga country to be
converted to pastoral lease. (*This was never granted.*)

16 DECEMBER 1940 — MONDAY
Left for Edith River country to muster.

19 DECEMBER 1940 — THURSDAY
Saw Quirke, the Manbulloo manager, and sold him 200
bullocks. Delivery at Manbulloo dependent on weather.

24 DECEMBER 1940 — TUESDAY
Down the river to Vampire Junction and up Vampire Creek.
Good few cattle about here but nearly all belong to
Boddington. Camped with Boddington up Vampire Creek.

1 JANUARY 1941 — WEDNESDAY
I was going to shift camp to Ashton Springs today but cattle
broke from the yard and got away. Put in the day tracking
them, got nearly all of them. About 100 head of cattle in
hand.

6 JANUARY 1941 — MONDAY
Mustered up Wandi Creek and across to Diamond
Billabong, got about 40 head of cattle, about half branded.
None of Gaden's cattle here.

10 JANUARY 1941 — FRIDAY
Telegram for me from Quirke, sent out from Pine Creek, to
meet him on train in Pine Creek today. Went to town but
Quirke did not arrive — a 24 mile ride for nothing.
Returned to the camp.

12 JANUARY 1941 — SUNDAY
Returned to the camp at Bon Rook junction; finished
mustering and will cut out tomorrow.

15 JANUARY 1941 — WEDNESDAY
Took cattle to Esmeralda. Drafted branders and started
branding and did 26. Heavy rain. Looks like raining all night.

27 JANUARY 1941 — MONDAY
Quirke inspected bullocks, rejected five, passed the rest.
Will start for Manbulloo Wednesday.

28 JANUARY 1941 — TUESDAY
Oiling up all the saddles, packs and gear. Got supplies for the
trip.

29 JANUARY 1941 — WEDNESDAY
Started for Manbulloo. Weather fine. Went to the Cullen
Yard.

1 FEBRUARY 1941 — SATURDAY
Horseshoe Creek. Watched cattle. Heavy storm. Cattle
rushed. Dropped one bullock, lame.

4 FEBRUARY 1941 — TUESDAY
Katherine. Swam cattle.

7 FEBRUARY 1941 — FRIDAY
Counted and gave delivery of cattle. Took train back to Pine
Creek.

17 FEBRUARY 1941 — MONDAY
Boarded *Marella* for Sydney.

SS MARELLA

21 FEBRUARY 1941

Dear Phil

I am on board the above boat — destination: Sydney, object
holiday — very much need it, too.

I had a letter from Mum some time ago, but I've lost it and
cannot remember the change of address. I will address this to
your last address in Wales and hope it reaches you.

I have been aboard a week and am enjoying it very much.
I've been going too long without a spell and, although I had
plenty of work on hand, I left my cow punchers to carry on and
booked my passage to Sydney.

As I suppose you know, I bought Esmeralda and a butchery,
this time last year. The butchery didn't pay, so I sold it in
September, and was glad to see the back of it.

I have sold a good few cattle. I sold 400 last May (mixed)
and I put about 120 bullocks through the shop. I sold about 100
bullocks to butchers and another 100 bullocks early this month
to Vesteys. So taking it by and large, it has turned out a fairly
good proposition.

The last mob of bullocks I sold, I had to drove them down to

Manbulloo Station, which, although only 60 miles, took me eight days. I had three rivers to cross and was lucky enough to get through, and only one was a swim. As it was February, I had the luck of a dead Chinaman to get through. We had to watch at night, of course, but I had six men and two good ones among them. One was my own head stockman and another chap I picked up and put on for the trip. It rained several nights and one night we had a particularly bad storm. It rained like hell, but the cattle just stuck their tails into the wind and never shifted. I was on watch nearly all night on my best night horse and was prepared for anything. Because of the thunder and lightning I was expecting them to gallop. I delivered three days later and delivered the full number, which was fairly good considering it was the middle of the wet.

However, I had had enough for a while, so I sent my plant back with my head stockman and told them to carry on yard building until I returned. I wired down to Burns Philp reserving a 1st class cabin, caught the train, hopped on the boat and here I am.

Unfortunately, I have to be back on the job by the second week in April as I have to have bullocks ready by the end of May. However, I am going to make the best of it.

I was going to fly down as it's 2000 miles from Darwin to Adelaide, and there are fast Lockheeds on that run that do it in a day. But I decided to go by boat as the trip is a great holiday, and a man can have a good loaf whether he likes it or not. These Burns Philp boats are very good to travel on; they are the Melbourne to Singapore run.

There is quite a good crowd on board, and owing to it being wartime, we are not full up. They are mostly Malay people — tin, rubber, teak and so on — and an army bloke or so, and some government officials.

I have developed a routine: morning tea 6.30, swim, gym, breakfast; then deck quoits or something of that nature, with a few beers at appropriate intervals; lunch, sleep till about 4.00; games and a few drinks till it's time to dress for dinner. The night is really the worst. The boat is blacked out and there are all sorts of regulations regarding portholes and lights and so on.

I am going to Sydney and will put a week or so in there. I have a lot of friends to look up and a book full of addresses, which I shall never get through. After a week or two in Sydney, I am going across to Victoria to stay with friends for the opening of the quail shooting season. From there, I'm going to Adelaide and then back up through Alice Springs to Pine Creek.

Write me as soon as you can and let me know what your address is and how you are all faring. Everyone out here is in very good spirits regarding the progress of the war. We appear to have done some good work in North Africa, which it is to be hoped we can follow up. The Aussies seem to be making a name for themselves . . .

With affection

ESMERALDA STATION
PINE CREEK
NORTHERN TERRITORY

10 AUGUST 1941

Dear Mum

I received your letter of June 6th a couple of days ago, a few days before another one, registered, and dated November 22nd. I am sending you the envelope to have a look at. It's certainly interesting. It has about six postmarks on it and has been all round Australia.

You seem to be having a pretty grim time over there; people over here hardly realise there's a war on. There is plenty of everything to eat and foodstuffs are fairly cheap, but clothing is very dear.

Cattle prices have risen a bit. The fat cattle market is fairly good, but this country of mine is not good enough to fatten cattle and I sell most of my bullocks as 'stores' (to be fattened). The 'store' market here is completely controlled by Vesteys, who won't give the grower more than a bare living. They are paying £3 per head for store bullocks that are delivered at one of their stations (Manbulloo), 60 miles from here. I have to drove them that 60 miles. It's a shocking price when you realise that fats are bringing up to £20 per head and more in some markets. I am starting to muster 200 bullocks for them now, but I hope it will be the last they get off me.

I am looking for some better country, country that will fatten and will be closer to a market. I hope this year to shift my herd off here. When I came back from south, I came up through the 'centre' and saw some very nice cattle country, but it's almost impossible to get country with water on it. Most of the creeks only hold for a few months after the 'wet', so that means boring, a very expensive business. Before the war it cost £1000 to put a bore down and equip it with windmill, tanks and a troughing, but I don't suppose you could do it for that now. £1000 isn't much when you say it quick, but just at present I've got an overdraft a kangaroo couldn't jump over. I'm getting used to that now though, in fact, I'd be lonely without one.

The boys are unlucky in losing their businesses. After battling a start and being more or less established, it must be heartbreaking. God alone knows what there will be to do after it's all over, or what we are going to use for money. I think a man with land will be better off than anybody; he will be able to grow something to eat.

I'm not doing as well here as I hoped. I don't see any prospect of doing any good unless I get out to a better district. I am trying to sell my buffalo shooting place. I don't know whether I'll be successful. It's pretty hard to sell anything to anyone now, and a damn sight harder to get money. I have several hundred pounds owing to me. I'm satisfied that getting blood out of stones is easy compared to separating some people from money.

I went out of the butchery with £105 on the books and have got precious little of that left. I sold a refrigerating plant 12 months ago and haven't been paid for it yet. I also have 150 quid to collect for bullocks, some of them sold over six months ago. I am leaving the day after tomorrow for a place called Marran-boy, about 100 miles from here, to buy 20 head of working horses and expect to have to pay cash for them.

However, I suppose I've got very little to complain about compared to some people. My brothers are all joined up or the equivalent. Nearly all my pals are in the army, navy or air force. I ought to be there too. I am not entirely out of it, and for that reason will not be accepted. More than that I cannot say at present.

I shall be looking forward to hearing from you again. I think the war position is considerably improved for us now, but things did look pretty bleak for us after the Crete show. The months are slowly creeping by and winter is on our side. I think there'll be chaos in Europe this winter.

The Morrises are well. Esma presented Fred with another son, which was some time ago. Well cheer up. I hope to get back to England as soon as it's all over.

Love to all, your loving son

1 NOVEMBER 1941 — SATURDAY
Left this morning with 73 head of horses and 160 head of cattle. Camped at Leichhardt.

2 DECEMBER 1941 — TUESDAY
Went across to Evelyn where the stock camp is mustering. About 80 head of cattle in hand. Instructed them to carry on mustering down the Mary.

25 DECEMBER 1941 — FRIDAY
Shifted camp across to Nine Mile. Water dry at yard. Dug a soak. Riley's camp is here. Yarded cattle and camped on water 3 miles away.

26 DECEMBER 1941 — FRIDAY
To station. Drafted branders.

27 DECEMBER 1941 — SATURDAY
Branded 22 calves, 11 males and 11 females. Camp spelling. I went with packs to Pine Creek for rations. Shortage of tucker could only get 1 bag flour.

SECRET

IMPERIAL GENERAL STAFF
(AUSTRALIAN SECTION)

ARMY HEADQUARTERS,
VICTORIA BARRACKS

I.R.C 16   MELBOURNE, 15th December, '41

Dear Sir,

    A personal note to let you know that
we at Army Headquarters have not forgotten
your existence. A large map, a little
red pin, a reference number, and you fit
into the scheme as one of "Australia's
Silent Guardians".

    As the end of another year draws to
a close, besides reminding you that you have
played an important part in the efficiency
of our Intelligence Organization, I desire
to express to you our appreciation of your
loyal and unselfish co-operation as a
M.R.O., and to convey to you the compliments
of the season.

    With best wishes,

        Yours sincerely,

        James A. Chapman

        Colonel,
Director of Military Intelligence.

4 JANUARY 1942 — SUNDAY
Left the cattle in charge of Cullen Richardson with five boys
and returned to Pine Creek. Will have to wait for rations.
No flour in town.

7 JANUARY 1942 — WEDNESDAY
Train from Darwin with R. Lee [the buyer of Esmeralda]
and E. Blackman [his manager] from Darwin. No flour
arrived.

8 JANUARY 1942 — THURSDAY
Borrowed some flour to carry on with. Left for station with
Lee and Blackman.

9 JANUARY 1942 — FRIDAY
Lee finished Esmeralda sale. Blackman to take over 21st.
Both returned to Pine Creek.

I saw an advertisement in the Government Gazette *for several
blocks of land with areas varying from six hundred square miles to
fifteen hundred. I put in an application for the medium sized thousand
square mile block and, being the only applicant, was successful. It was
on the Barkly Tablelands, a much more attractive proposition than my
own property, Esmeralda Station, which was about fifteen hundred
square miles of rough and scrubby country. The downs country had
much better quality grass and was closer to the markets. However, to
muster my herd and move them down was a very big undertaking.
Consequently I invited a cattleman friend, Jack Guild, to join me
whose property, the Veldt, was also rough breeding country. We took
a combined herd of seventeen hundred head of cattle, together with
eighty horses, twelve packs and a wagonette for carrying enough
rations to feed ten or twelve stockmen. The arrangement was that I
would muster my herd and bring them to his property, which was
about a hundred and fifty miles south on the way to the new block.*

17 FEBRUARY 1942 — TUESDAY
Started cattle this morning in charge of Cullen Richardson,
Willie Riley and four boys. Waybills signed, 492 cattle, 25
plant horses. Left cattle at Bon Rook and returned to Pine
Creek and camped.

22 FEBRUARY 1942 — SUNDAY
Packed up to get away.

2 MARCH 1942 — MONDAY
Went on with cattle and camped Eight Mile. Very little
water. Cattle thirsty.

3 MARCH 1942 — TUESDAY
Bad camp last night, cattle dry. Went on this morning.
Watered at Bullocks Head. Camped at Maude Creek, J.
Jordon caught me up here today. Put him on cooking.

8 MARCH 1942 — SUNDAY
Arrived Veldt. Counted cattle and paddocked them. Three
short.

13 MARCH 1942 — FRIDAY
W. Moore started at £7 per week and keep (drovers hand).
We left with 1700 head of mixed cattle, 81 plant horses and
12 packs. W. Moore in charge of cattle and seven boys.
Travelled 3 miles and camped. Jack Guild came as far as the
camp and returned to station. Mrs Guild to leave for south
tomorrow because of war.

*The cattle had to be watched all night for the first two or three days.
Once they settled down and got used to being watched one man could
hold them easily. I knew that I was going to have problems with
water as there were some long dry stretches in front of me. I had also
heard there were a couple of mobs of bullocks on the road which would
seriously deplete the bores.*

15 MARCH 1942 — SUNDAY

Some cattle got away last night. Billy Moore tracked them up and got them. Went on to the Stirling River.

22 MARCH 1942 — SUNDAY

Watered cattle and horses and went out about four miles and camped. Twenty-five miles to No. 1 bore.

23 MARCH 1942 — MONDAY

Got a good start this morning, but buggy wheel broke. Lost three hours repairing it. Caught cattle on dinner camp. Passed Alec Grant and Norman Stay with bullocks for Mataranka trucks.

24 MARCH 1942 — TUESDAY

Reached the cattle camp at two o'clock this morning. Got an hour's sleep and started them off. Watered the buggy horses. Went on to the bore for another load of water and back to the cattle. Camped four miles out. Should make water about nine or ten o'clock tomorrow morning. Cattle very thirsty.

25 MARCH 1942 — WEDNESDAY

Got the lead of the cattle into the bore at 8.30 this morning. Tank went dry after watering 1200 head, 500 head still to be watered. The next water is 14 miles, so position is serious. Camped them in the heat of the day. Sent Moore on with the dry mob. Packed up and brought the droving plant horses, packs and wagonette and rest of the cattle. Caught up with Moore 5 miles out, camped.

26 MARCH 1942 — THURSDAY

Pushed the cattle off before daybreak. Two hours away. Sent one boy back for them and took the droving plant on. Cattle got a bit of suck at a small water hole. Mad with thirst. Pushed them on to another larger hole and got them half a drink of muddy water. Water more plentiful along here. Got them another drink at sundown and camped. Jack Guild caught us up.

THE NORTHERN TERRITORY OF AUSTRALIA.

Form Q.

The *Brands Ordinance* 1928.

WAYBILL ———————— OF TRAVELLING STOCK.

I,* _Thomas Ernest Cole_ ....declare that ~~I am~~ *we*.
(or _T. C. Cole and J. H. Gunba_ ....are *is*) the owners of the Travelling
Stock described hereunder, and I further declare the Stock to be started this day
by _me_ ....
from _The Veldt Station_ ...., will be driven to _Tandigee_ ....
by the following route, namely _overland stock route_ ....
and will be ~~delivered there to~~ _grazed on block 2 subdivision of Newcastle Water_

No. of Stock.	Description of Stock.	Sex.	Brands and Marks.	Health.
2	Various ages and sex	F	VLT JTJ earmark A.J.3.	
1	" " "	F	~~VLT~~ F.2.	
325	" " " "		VLT earmark AJ3	
200	" " " "		TGW earmark E.6.6.	
100	" " " "		SMT " A.S.	
150	" " " "		MST " F.2.	
100	" " " "		TSN " AJ.4	
400	" " " "		♀ " A S	
50	" " " "		⚷ " B K.6.	
75	" " " "		⚳ " A V S	
300	calves at foot unbranded			
2	cows		OTT earmark E46.	
1705				

Waybill for travelling stock from the Veldt Station to Tandidgee Station.

1 APRIL 1942 — WEDNESDAY

All the boys left about 12.30 this morning and let the cattle
go in the second watch. Jack Guild, Moore and myself
mustered all night. We got nearly all of them by daylight.
Rode into Birdum to try and get men. Engaged several boys,
to be at camp tomorrow.

*There were only three of us to muster seventeen hundred head of cattle
that had walked off in the middle of the night. Fortunately they had
kept together and we managed to get them in hand.*

2 APRIL 1942 — THURSDAY

One boy turned up this morning, the rest jibbed on it. Back
to Birdum again. Got a promise from three boys.

3 APRIL 1942 — FRIDAY

Got away this morning with four boys and one halfcaste,
George Cummings. Camped Six Mile.

4 APRIL 1942 — SATURDAY

Dry camp, four or five miles from Ironstone Bore. Althaus
passed with six hundred bullocks.

25 APRIL 1942 — SATURDAY

Left No. 7 dry camped about three miles out on the Sturt Plain.

*The weather turned intensely hot as I was faced with a long stretch
over the Sturt Plain with not a single shade tree. I had a hard twenty
miles to go and it turned out to be the hardest stretch of the entire trip.*

26 APRIL 1942 — SUNDAY

Very hot day. About eight head of cattle perished crossing
the Sturt Plain. Dropped others. Camped Crawford's Grave.

27 APRIL 1942 — MONDAY
Watered at North Newcastle and camped on the Five Mile
Creek.

28 APRIL 1942 — TUESDAY
Camped about a mile and a half from Newcastle Waters.
Understand Tandidgee is dry and expect to have difficulties
over water.

30 APRIL 1942 — THURSDAY
Left and camped mile and half from water. J. Jordon started
cooking at £1 per day.

1 MAY 1942 — FRIDAY
Watered in Newcastle Creek and camped on the edge of the
plain, 5 miles out.

2 MAY 1942 — SATURDAY
Dry camped, 5 miles this side of No. 8 bore.

4 MAY 1942 — MONDAY
Dry camped mile and half from bore.

5 MAY 1942 — TUESDAY
Reached No. 7 on boundary. Watered cattle and let them
go. Paid off Moore and boys; J. Jordon finished as drover's
cook.

*It was seventy three days since I left Esmeralda and it was with
tremendous relief that I turned the cattle out on the plain of Mitchell
and Flinders grass at Tandidgee.*

6 MAY 1942 — WEDNESDAY
J. Jordon started as camp cook at £3 10s per week. Kept on
two boys, Bruce and Charlie.

7 MAY 1942 — THURSDAY
Left after dinner for Newcastle Waters for mail, rations, and
boys, if possible. Moore also packed up and left. Camped
No. 8 bore.

TANDIDGEE STATION
NEWCASTLE WATERS
NORTHERN TERRITORY

1 AUGUST 1942

Dear Mum

Your letter of March 22nd I received last week and was very
glad to hear from you. I also got a bundle of papers about a
month before that. Did you send them? They may have come
from Peg. No letter though!

As you will see, I have a new address. I sold Esmeralda,
unstocked, and took up 100 square miles on the Barkly Tablelands.
It is extra good grazing country, some of the best land in Australia.

I have gone into partnership with another chap and we have
put 2000 head of cattle onto the place to start it off. I moved all
the cattle I could muster (I missed a lot) off Esmeralda, and he
cleaned his place up and 2000 head of mixed cattle is the result.

I sent the Esmeralda cattle down to his place in two mobs. I
took them over myself from Katherine to The Veldt (my
partner's place). I was at Katherine, swimming the second mob
across the river, when I got your cable.

From The Veldt I took the first mob down to the new
property. We started with 1700 and I was 54 days on the road
and had a very bad trip. We had a light wet season and I had to
get over several dry stages; also the mob was a bit big and
unwieldy. As a matter of fact, 1000 head of mixed cattle is
plenty big enough. However, we wanted to get as many down
to Newcastle Waters as soon as we could. As owing to the bad
season, the stock route would be getting worse, particularly
with other mobs of cattle travelling about it. Later on, Jack
Guild brought 350 and arrived here July 2nd.

Tandidgee Station.
Newcastle Waters
N.T.
Australia
Aug 1st 1942

Dear Mum
          Your letter of March 22nd received
last week & very glad to hear from you.
I also got a bundle of papers about a
month before that. Did you send them? They
May have come from Peg. No letter tho'.
As you will see I have a new address.
I sold Esmeralda, unstocked, & took up
a thousand square miles on the Barkly
Tableland. Extra good grazing country,
some of the best in Australia. I have
gone into partnership with another chap &
we have put two thousand head of
cattle on to the block to start it off.
I shifted all the cattle I could muster
(I missed a lot) off Esmeralda & he
cleaned his place up & 2,000 head of
mixed cattle is the result. I took sent
the Esmeralda cattle down to his place in
two mobs & was at Katherine, swimming
them across the river when I got your cable.
That was the second mob. I took them over
myself from the Katherine to The Veldt (my
partners place). From The Veldt I took the
first mob down to the new property. We

We have an extra good block of country here, although now it is short of water — owing to the rotten 'wet' we had — the water holes are all dry. At present our cattle are watering on sub-artesian bores, of which we have two on the property.

It is much better country than Esmeralda, which as a matter of fact wasn't much good. Esmeralda had plenty of water but very poor grazing. It would grow cattle but wouldn't fatten, also it was very rough and the cattle were never really in hand. I was very lucky to get a buyer and damn glad to get out of it.

The cattle are all very poor now as the droving down has knocked the condition off them, but we expect to have some good bullocks ready to go off next year.

This war is getting worse and worse now that we have lost Tobruk. Len was there, did he get out all right? I am anxious to hear. I don't think there is a ghost of a chance of the war ending this year — unless we are beaten. Both Japan and America, particularly the latter, are fresh, so I can't see it ending inside another three years.

The European part may end before that. The civil population will crack first, especially in countries where the winters are severe.

We are good for another three or four years here and, so far nobody has had to suffer any inconvenience, although they are starting to feel the pinch. Tea and clothes are rationed. I think we will have to carry a fair amount of weight from now on — they are making an effort to harness everything up now and people can't do just as they like.

Australia is going to be tremendously strong when the Americans are consolidated. There are a lot of them here. However, the Japs may tackle us and if they do — these Northern Rivers will be running — and it won't be water.

I shall most likely be well in it before long. I have been trying to join up but they won't take cattle men. The cattle industry is essential; there are a lot of Americans to feed and bullocks are a bit short. There are plenty in the Territory of course, but owing to the shortage of labour we are having a job to get them down to the southern markets. The stock route to

Queensland goes through this place and 20 000 bullocks have passed since I've been here, travelling in mobs of from 1000 to 1500.

I am hoping to be able to make the trip home after the war. I would like to bring you out here for a holiday; I think you would like it, if only for the change. We hope to get a decent homestead built here eventually, but just at present can't buy a sheet of iron or a pound of nails and as for fencing wire, it's an impossibility. I had two tons and the army grabbed it. However, we'll manage somehow. Jack Guild is married and has a mob of kids (I forget how many). His wife is in Adelaide with most of the children. I don't s'pose she will get back till after the war.

Well, I will say goodbye. God knows when you will get this.

With love

WYNDHAM
WESTERN AUSTRALIA

29 MARCH 1943

Dear Mum

Your last letter of November 1st, I'm ashamed to say, I've had some time. I've had so much to do that I've been postponing answering it until I could settle down comfortably. I am writing from Wyndham, Western Australia.

I came across to inspect some cattle and having done that I am trying to get down to Perth by plane. I have some business to do and will try and combine it with a short holiday. I've had my nose to the grindstone for over two years without a break. From Perth I will probably go across to Adelaide and back through Alice Springs.

I wrote to Len — that is the second letter I've written him — perhaps he didn't get mine or perhaps I didn't get his reply.

I don't know who the chap could be that claimed to know me. I don't think he did. I've never had a nickname and I was one of the most well-known men in the Territory up to the outbreak of war — quite a lot of blokes have claimed to have been out buffalo shooting with me who've never even seen me — that nickname is sheer imagination.

I had a letter from Fred Morris recently. He is an intelligence officer and is somewhere outside Sydney. Mrs Morris is living in a suburb of Sydney. She lost pretty well everything after the first air-raid on Darwin. She was evacuated with precious little beyond the clothes she stood up in. Her address is: 49 Tranmere Street, Drummoyne Sydney NSW.

Buffalo shooting is a thing of the past since war broke out — can't get cartridges or transport. I haven't fired a shot since '39.

I still own Kapalga. It is my own. I went into partnership with Guild only with the cattle. He owned a place called The Veldt and I had 1000 square miles of country out from Newcastle and all the Esmeralda stock and plant. (I had previously sold the Esmeralda leases.) He shifted all his stock from The Veldt and I shifted all my stock down from Pine Creek. Later, we sold The Veldt leases in which I had a half share. Kapalga will be a good proposition after the war, and, if I don't shoot, it will be readily saleable.

At Tandidgee (the new place) we are handicapped in several directions. It is first-class grazing country, but short of water and we have to get bores put down. There is the greatest difficulty getting materials, such as pumping equipment, bore casing, piping, troughing, etc., and owing to the depth the borer has to go, it is also very expensive. We estimate the cost of one bore, fully equipped, at £2000. We could do with about £10 000, then we could make a valuable property out of it in a very short time. As it is, all the improvements will have to come out of the place itself. We can only borrow £2000 from the bank, which is just enough to get us into trouble. I can see years of work ahead of us. Eventually, no doubt, we will have a valuable place but it will be a slow weary business.

My health is splendid, and always is. When I am on the station my weight is down around ten stone ten. Riding does this to my weight, but it goes up to about 12 stone if I am off a horse for very long and enjoying a bit of soft living.

I have just finished a very interesting trip, although, it is actually more interesting to look back on. I rode from Tandidgee, Newcastle Waters, to the Western Australia border — a distance of about 450 miles the way that I went. I saw a great variety of country and renewed a number of old friendships among the station men. I took one boy with me, who took off after I got about 100 miles out. I also took two packs and eight horses, altogether. I got on quite well. When I got to the Western Australia border I was able to get a truck into Wyndham, so I sold my horses, packs and saddles. I was sorry in a way as I had two of my best horses with me, Star and Spark. Spark is the best horse I've ever bred and one of the best I've ever ridden.

Well, there is nothing more to write about. I hope to be in Perth shortly. I cannot make any reference to times or schedules or route. The distance from here is 2000 miles.

When I get to Perth I will have been all around Australia and crossed it from East to West and from North to South.

Love to all, your affectionate son, Tom